DEEPENING YOUR ROOTS

in God's Family

This book belongs to: _____

DEEPENING YOUR ROOTS
in God's Family

THE 2:7 SERIES

2

NAVPRESS
Discipleship Inside Out®

CDM
CHURCH DISCIPLESHIP MINISTRY

Discipleship Inside Out®

NavPress is the publishing ministry of The Navigators, an international Christian organization and leader in personal spiritual development. NavPress is committed to helping people grow spiritually and enjoy lives of meaning and hope through personal and group resources that are biblically rooted, culturally relevant, and highly practical.

**For a free catalog go to www.NavPress.com
or call 1.800.366.7788 in the United States or 1.800.839.4769 in Canada.**

ACKNOWLEDGMENT

We are grateful for the dedicated efforts of Ron Oertli, who originated the concept of THE 2:7 SERIES and is its principal author. Ron is also the key person responsible for this updated edition. This discipleship training approach began in Denver in 1970 and continues to be highly effective in many places around the world.

CONTENTS

MY COMPLETION RECORD

As you complete each item, ask someone in your group to sign off for that item with his or her initials and the calendar date.

SCRIPTURE MEMORY	INITIALS	DATE
Required verses: "Live the New Life"		
"Christ the Center"—2 Corinthians 5:17		
"Obedience to Christ"—Romans 12:1		
"The Word"—2 Timothy 3:16		
"Prayer"—John 15:7		
"Fellowship"—Hebrews 10:24-25		
"Witnessing"—Matthew 4:19		
Recommended but optional verses: "Live the New Life"		
"Christ the Center"—Galatians 2:20		
"Obedience to Christ"—John 14:21		
"The Word"—Joshua 1:8		
"Prayer"—Philippians 4:6-7		
"Fellowship"—1 John 1:3		
"Witnessing"—Romans 1:16		
Quote the six "Live the New Life" required verses		
Quote all 12 "Live the New Life" verses		
Quote your memory verses from book 1		
Reviewed the book 1 memory verses for 14 consecutive days		
Completed the Scripture Memory Principles Quiz on page 19		
Completed the Self-Checking Quiz on pages 46–47		
QUIET TIME		
Completed *My Reading Highlights* for 14 consecutive days		
WITNESS		
Enjoyed a relating activity (page 54)		
Told "My Story" from an outline in less than 4 minutes		
BIBLE STUDY		
Session 2—Maturing in Christ (pages 19–24)		
Session 3—Spiritual Warfare (pages 33–36)		
Session 4—Faith and the Truths of God (pages 40–44)		
Session 5—Knowing God's Will (pages 48–52)		
Session 6—Walking as a Servant (pages 55–59)		
GROUP EXERCISE		
Participated in an Extended Time with God		

OTHER		
Read and marked "Relationship Evangelism" (pages 26–33)		
Read and marked *My Heart — Christ's Home* (pages 83–90)		
Completed pages 91–92		
Read "Suggestions for Your Extended Time with God" (pages 93–105)		
LEADER'S CHECK		
Graduated from *Deepening Your Roots in God's Family* (book 2)		

ABBREVIATIONS FOR BIBLE VERSIONS

Unless otherwise identified, all Scripture quotations in this publication are taken from the *Holy Bible, New International Version* (NIV). You can refer to this list when you encounter unfamiliar Bible version abbreviations.

- (AMP) The Amplified Bible
- (ESV) English Standard Version
- (KJV) King James Version
- (MLB) Modern Language Bible: The Berkeley Version in Modern English
- (MSG) The Message
- (NASB) New American Standard Bible
- (NCV) New Century Version
- (NIV) New International Version
- (NKJV) New King James Version
- (NLT) New Living Translation
- (NRSV) New Revised Standard Version
- (PH) The New Testament in Modern English (J. B. Phillips)

SESSION 1

OUTLINE OF THIS SESSION

1. Open the session in prayer.
2. Go over "Reviewing the Goals of Book 1 in The 2:7 Series" (pages 9–10).
3. Preview book 2 by looking over *My Completion Record* (pages 7–8).
4. Will you memorize in the same translation you used in book 1?
5. Survey "Scripture Memory Guide—Week 1" (pages 10–11).
6. Read aloud "The *TMS* in Book 2" and "Bible Study in Book 2" (pages 11–12).
7. Read and discuss "Principles for Memorizing Scripture" (page 13).
8. Discuss "Practical Suggestions on Prayer" (pages 14–15). Locate prayer sheets at the end of this book (pages 141–146).
9. Read "Assignment for Session 2" (page 16).
10. Close the session in prayer.

REVIEWING THE GOALS OF BOOK 1 IN THE 2:7 SERIES

The goals of book 1 were:

1. To enjoy Bible reading by:
   a. Using a contemporary translation or paraphrase
   b. Using a method of Bible marking
2. To successfully memorize the five key Scripture memory verses contained in *Beginning with Christ* and to have the option of memorizing an outreach verse
3. To experience more consistent and meaningful quiet times by:
   a. Combining meaningful Bible reading and prayer
   b. Succeeding in having seven consecutive quiet times during the course
   c. Recording daily quiet time thoughts on a *My Reading Highlights* page
4. To study and discuss The Wheel Illustration
5. To study and discuss *Tyranny of the Urgent*
6. To understand the value of The Wheel and The Hand Illustrations

7. To come to a deeper conviction about reasons for memorizing Scripture and to identify possible hindrances to doing well in Scripture memory
8. To establish an evangelism prayer list

SCRIPTURE MEMORY GUIDE—WEEK 1

EXCERPTS FROM THE *TOPICAL MEMORY SYSTEM* (*TMS*)

You Can Memorize Scripture!

Your Memory Is Good. Do you think you have a poor memory? Wait a minute. What's your address and phone number? How about all that information you know by heart about your job? How about all the people you call by name? Or the facts and figures you can recite about your favorite sport or hobby? You see, your memory is really pretty good after all. Anything is easy to memorize when you are really interested in it, or use it often.

Attitude Makes the Difference. A good memory is not something you either have or don't have. It is a skill, and like other skills it can be improved. Attitude can make the difference. Adopt an attitude of confidence in Scripture memory and it will help your memory work.

Count on God's Help. Here's some additional encouragement: You can count on God to help you memorize Scripture, for He wants His Word to be in the hearts of His children. "These commandments that I give you today are to be on your hearts" (Deuteronomy 6:6); "let the message of Christ dwell among you richly" (Colossians 3:16).

Why the Topics?

In book 1, you learned the topics and references as well as the verses. Here in book 2, you will do the same.

Two important reasons for knowing the topics of verses you memorize are:

1. The topics help you understand the verses and make them easier to memorize and review.
2. The topics give you mental hooks with which to draw a particular verse from memory when you need it. They help you call the right verse to mind when meditating, witnessing, counseling, doing Bible study, or preparing a talk.

So familiarize yourself with the "Live the New Life" topics on page 11 and learn each topic along with the verses.

Scripture Memory Helps in Book 2

The weekly Scripture memory guides in this course help in four areas:

1. How we can *memorize* Scripture verses more easily

2. How to *apply* the verses to our lives

3. How to *review* them so we can have them at our fingertips

4. How to *continue* memorizing Scripture after finishing this course

THE *TMS* IN BOOK 2

As you may know, NavPress publishes a Scripture memory course called the *Topical Memory System* (*TMS*). (Over the next few years you might choose to complete the *TMS*). The whole course contains sixty verses grouped into five major topics:

A. *Live the New Life*	12 verses
B. *Proclaim Christ*	12 verses
C. *Rely on God's Resources*	12 verses
D. *Be Christ's Disciple*	12 verses
E. *Grow in Christlikeness*	12 verses

Each topic (A through E) has six subtopics. All the verses deal with important areas of the Christian life. You can find more Scripture memory information at www.2-7series.org.

During book 2, you will memorize verses from "Live the New Life." Notice that the topics are the same important subjects you discussed in your Bible studies during book 1.

A. Live The New Life	Required:	Recommended but Optional:
Christ the Center	2 Corinthians 5:17	Galatians 2:20
Obedience to Christ	Romans 12:1	John 14:21
The Word	2 Timothy 3:16	Joshua 1:8
Prayer	John 15:7	Philippians 4:6-7
Fellowship	Hebrews 10:24-25	1 John 1:3
Witnessing	Matthew 4:19	Romans 1:16

Probably your first question is "Do I need to memorize all twelve of these great verses to graduate from book 2?" Or "How could I possibly memorize twelve verses during this course? It stretched me to memorize the verses in book 1!" The straight answer is that you can graduate from book 2 by perfectly quoting one verse on each of the six topics—that is, six memory verses.

But quoting all twelve is highly recommended.

Thousands of people have found memorizing twelve verses in book 2 to be easier than memorizing the verses in book 1. They learned to apply the principles for memorizing and reviewing Scripture verses. They continued to review the verse cards they already knew. Then they focused on learning one new verse (phrase by phrase) over a two-day period. They continued to review that verse, preferably more than once a day. Then over two more days, they memorized the second verse. That left them three days to continue to review the two new verses before their next weekly 2:7 group. This is doable!

Give yourself a gift! Go for the twelve verses while you are with friends in a positive Scripture-memory environment. It is a relatively small investment that can pay huge dividends. If you follow proven Scripture-memory principles and guidelines, it will happen for you as it has for so many others.

BIBLE STUDY IN BOOK 2

The Bible is a book of life, a treasure chest of truth . . .

> refreshing the soul . . .
> making wise the simple . . .
> giving joy to the heart . . .
> giving light to the eyes . . .
> more precious than gold . . .
> sweeter than honey. (Psalm 19:7-11)

The abundant wisdom and riches God has provided in His Word are available to every Christian, but they are only experienced by those who persistently dig for them. Meditation and prayer are two keys that unlock this storehouse of God's wisdom as you study. Prayerfully meditating on each verse you look up helps you grasp its meaning and its application for everyday life.

As you continue to walk with Christ, you may wonder what God's plan and purpose is for your life and how you can best walk by faith. During this course, your Bible studies cover five important subjects concerning your walk with Christ:

- Maturing in Christ
- Spiritual Warfare
- Faith and the Truths of God
- Knowing God's Will
- Walking as a Servant

PRINCIPLES FOR MEMORIZING SCRIPTURE

AS YOU START TO MEMORIZE THE VERSE

1. Study the Scripture memory guide each week. You will find it extremely helpful.
2. It helps to read the verses before and after a memory verse—that is, the context or setting of the verse.
3. Get a clear understanding of the meaning of each verse. Perhaps read the verse in another translation or paraphrase for clarity.
4. Read the verse thoughtfully, aloud or in a whisper. Look at the verse as a whole. Each time you read it, say the topic, reference, verse, and reference.
5. Discuss the verse with God in prayer. Ask Him for insight and appropriate application.

WHILE YOU ARE MEMORIZING THE VERSE

6. Learn the topic, reference, and first phrase as one unit.
7. After learning the topic, reference, and first phrase, continue to add one phrase at a time until you can say the whole verse.
8. Work on the verse aloud as often as possible.
9. As you memorize and review the verse, think about how it applies to your own life and daily circumstances.
10. Always include the topic and reference at the beginning and the reference at the end.
11. One excellent habit to form is to use spare moments during the day (such as while waiting, walking, or driving) to review or meditate on verses.

AFTER YOU CAN SAY THE TOPIC, REFERENCE, VERSE, AND REFERENCE CORRECTLY

12. Review the verse frequently (even several times a day) in the first few days after learning it. This plants it solidly in your mind.
13. After you learn the verse, write it out or quote it to someone, deepening that early impression on your mind.
14. Review, review, review! Repetition is the best method for strengthening your grasp on the verses you have memorized. It helps you maintain your ability to quote them.

PRACTICAL SUGGESTIONS ON PRAYER

A SUGGESTED PRAYER FORMAT: ACTS OR CATS

The disciples asked Jesus Christ to teach them how to pray (Luke 11:1-4). He gave them a pattern that began with praise and adoration and ended with supplication.

One helpful way to follow this pattern is to use the acrostic ACTS (adoration, confession, thanksgiving, supplication). Some prefer to take care of confession first before continuing their prayer time: CATS.

Please look up the following verses and write a summary thought for each:

Adoration: praising God's character and attributes.

    1 Chronicles 29:11 _____

    Psalm 145:1-3 _____

Confession: confessing our sins to God (some prefer to do this first).

    Psalm 32:5 _____

    Job 42:5-6 _____

Thanksgiving: expressing our gratitude to God.

    Ephesians 5:20 _____

    Psalm 100:4 _____

Supplication: a humble prayer to God, asking for ourselves or for others.

    Matthew 7:7-8 _____

    James 4:2 _____

This prayer format is an approach you may use for a week or two and then change to another pattern. A few weeks later, you might want to return to it. It is to use as much or as little as you choose.

> Devote yourselves to prayer, being watchful and thankful.
> —COLOSSIANS 4:2

USING PRAYER SHEETS

You can find blank prayer sheets at the end of this book. They are also available along with other downloads at www.2-7series.org.

It is a great encouragement to see answers to prayer. Recording how God has answered alerts us to His working and reminds us to be thankful. We can expect answers to our prayers that are in line with His will (1 John 5:14-15).

Not every prayer request we pray needs to be written down on a prayer sheet. You can record requests that you want to bring to the Lord repeatedly: life issues, family, ministry, job, and so on. Be specific in your prayers. Be bold. Follow the counsel of Hebrews 4:16: "Let us then approach God's throne of grace with confidence, so that we may receive mercy and find grace to help us in our time of need."

State your request so that you can tell when God has answered. It is difficult to identify a specific answer for a vague request. You will find it helpful and encouraging to record requests and their answers.

Here is a sample of how someone made entries on a prayer sheet:

REQUEST	GOD'S ANSWER
2/4 floor covering for the basement at a reasonable price	5/20 $14—carpet and pad for only $1.95/sq. yard
2/10 Membership in the right church for us	3/16 Confirmed that Westside Church is for us
2/13 Someone to start discipling by March 15	5/12 George seems to be the one!
3/10 Christian friend for 10-year-old Mark	6/20 Perez family moved next door—their son is 12
3/28 That Bill Alden would finish the TMS	
4/17 To be close friends with George and Mary	
5/4 Extra money to attend July conference	6/8 Garage sale brought in $302
5/10 Jerry Cole would get a job in the Middle East	
5/11 Safe delivery and a healthy baby for Al and Nancy	6/8 Seth Allen arrived in good health
5/31 Close friendship with Don S.	

ASSIGNMENT FOR SESSION 2

1. Scripture Memory: Study and complete "Scripture Memory Guide—Week 2" (pages 17–18). Memorize the verse(s) on "Christ the Center": 2 Corinthians 5:17 and Galatians 2:20 (recommended but optional). In preparation for the "Scripture Memory Principles Quiz" during session 2, review "Principles for Memorizing Scripture" (page 13). During the quiz, you need to list only six of the principles of Scripture memory in order to get signed off on *My Completion Record*. However, you are probably thinking that it would be wise to be able to recall more than six, to allow yourself a little margin. (It is okay to paraphrase and abbreviate your six or more entries.)

2. Quiet Time: Continuing to use *My Reading Highlights* and *My Reading Progress* can help you enjoy Bible reading and marking as you did in book 1.

3. Bible Study: Please complete the Bible study "Maturing in Christ" (pages 19–24).

4. Other:

   a. You want to start using a prayer sheet to record your requests and God's answers. In session 4, we will discuss how this has worked for everyone in the group.

   b. Please bring your evangelism prayer list to class.

   c. Come ready to have several items initialed on *My Completion Record*.

SESSION 2

OUTLINE OF THIS SESSION

1. Open the session in prayer.
2. Break into verse review groups and quote the verse(s) on "Christ the Center": 2 Corinthians 5:17 and Galatians 2:20 (recommended but optional). Also review the memory verses from book 1.
3. Share some quiet-time thoughts from *My Reading Highlights*.
4. Complete the "Scripture Memory Principles Quiz" (page 19).
5. Discuss the continued use of an evangelism prayer list.
6. Survey the "Scripture Memory Guide—Week 2" (pages 17–18).
7. Discuss the Bible study "Maturing in Christ" (pages 19–24).
8. Read "Assignment for Session 3" (page 24).
9. Close the session in prayer.

SCRIPTURE MEMORY GUIDE—WEEK 2

Off to a Good Start

You have chosen the translation you want to use for your memory work in book 2, perhaps the same one you used in book 1. You have some memory cards ready to go.

Scripture Memory Guide

Each week, the Scripture memory guide gives you two helpful sections:

1. **About the Verses**—makes the verses more meaningful and easier to learn and apply.
2. **Your Weekly Plan**—gives you suggestions on how to manage your memory work.

About the Verses

LIVE THE NEW LIFE

Every person has physical life. When we have received Jesus Christ into our lives as Savior and Lord, we then possess a new spiritual life—the life of Christ in us.

This new life may be illustrated by a wheel, as we saw in book 1 (pages 49–53). A wheel gets its motivating force from the hub. In the Christian life, Christ is the hub, the source of power and motivation for living for Him (John 15:5). He lives in us in the person of the Holy Spirit, whose main purpose is to glorify Christ.

The rim of the wheel represents you, the Christian, responding to Christ's lordship through your wholehearted obedience to Him. Such obedience is linked with every other element of the Christ-centered life.

The spokes of the wheel show the means by which Christ's power reaches our lives. The vertical spokes symbolize our relationship to God. The horizontal spokes represent our relationships with other people, both believers and unbelievers. The wheel functions smoothly only when all the spokes are present and in proper balance.

TOPIC 1: CHRIST THE CENTER

Just as the driving force in a wheel comes from the hub, so the power to live the Christian life comes from Christ. It is not our resolve to "turn over a new leaf" but rather our active dependence on Him that enables us to live lives that are pleasing to God.

2 Corinthians 5:17—Life in Christ is completely new, and His presence gives an entirely new dimension to it. Our old ambitions, outlook, and values are changed as we come to know Him and as His power becomes operative in our lives.

Galatians 2:20 (recommended but optional)—Not only are we in Christ, but He lives in us. These two truths teach us the closeness of the relationship we enjoy with Him. As believers, we are identified with Him in His death and in His resurrected life. By faith we rely on Him in order to live His life in and through us.

Your Weekly Plan

1. Download and print Scripture memory cards for this course, or on one side of a blank card write the topic, reference, verse, and reference. On side two write only the topic and reference. Have a card for each verse you plan to memorize this week.

2. Start memorizing 2 Corinthians 5:17, quoting the topic and reference and then adding one phrase at a time until you can quote the whole verse. When you are memorizing two verses in one week, you want to memorize the first verse in two days, then the second verse in two days, leaving three days to review them (more than once a day if possible).

3. Each day you want to quote aloud the verses you memorized in book 1 along with your new memory verse(s).

4. Plan to carry your verse cards with you so you can use spare moments during the day to memorize, review, and meditate on your verses.

5. Many have found that the best times to work on a new verse are just before going to bed or soon after getting up in the morning.

6. Before meeting with your group for session 3, you can deepen your recall by writing out your new verses or by quoting them to someone.

> I seek you with all my heart;
>   do not let me stray from your commands.
> I have hidden your word in my heart
>   that I might not sin against you. . . .
> I meditate on your precepts
>   and consider your ways.
> —Psalm 119:10-11,15

SCRIPTURE MEMORY PRINCIPLES QUIZ

From what you studied on page 13, list at least six principles of Scripture memory. You may summarize or paraphrase—you don't need to quote them exactly.

_____

_____

_____

_____

_____

_____

_____

_____

_____

_____

_____

_____

_____

_____

MATURING IN CHRIST

The twenty-first-century world is characterized by rapid change. Increasingly, technological advances are providing instant communication via satellite, Internet, phone, and instant information stored and transmitted by high-speed computers. We are a generation that has come to expect and demand everything "now." Christians must remember, however, that there is no such thing as "instant maturity" in the Christian experience. Becoming a Christian begins a lifelong adventure of knowing God better and loving Him more.

> Don't let the world around you squeeze you into its own mould, but let God re-make you so that your whole attitude of mind is changed. Thus you will prove in practice that the will of [God is] good, acceptable to him and perfect.
>
> —ROMANS 12:2 (PH)

THINK ABOUT:

What are some similarities between physical and spiritual development?

MOVING TOWARD MATURITY

1. You took your first step toward spiritual maturity when you put your faith in Christ. Read Ephesians 4:11-16.

    a. What is God's desire for you (verses 13,15)? _____

    _____

    b. What are some characteristics of immature Christians ("children" or "infants"; verse 14)? _____

    _____

    c. According to this passage, what characterizes a spiritually mature person? _____

    _____

    _____

2. In this chart, contrast a person's old nature with the Christian's new nature (Ephesians 4:22-24).

Old Nature	New Nature

3. Consider 2 Corinthians 3:18.

    a. Into whose image are you being changed? _____

    b. Who brings about this change? _____

    c. How rapidly do you think change usually occurs? _____

    _____

d. How complete will the change finally be? _____

_____

4. What do the following verses in Romans tell you about your relationship to Christ?

   a. What has already happened to you (5:8-9)? _____

   _____

   b. What should you be doing (6:19)? _____

   _____

   c. What can you expect in the future (8:16-18)? _____

   _____

These three aspects of salvation in Christ (justification, sanctification, and glorification) are helpful in understanding God's plan for believers.

Justification (*event*)	Past tense—I have been saved from the penalty of sin.	My position is in Christ.
Sanctification (*process*)	Present tense—I am being saved from the power of sin.	My condition is becoming like Christ.
Glorification (*expectation*)	Future tense—I will be saved from the presence of sin	My expectation is to be like Christ.

YOUR STARTING POINT

5. Examine Colossians 2:6-7.

   a. How did you begin your life in Christ? _____

   _____

   b. How should you continue to grow? _____

   _____

6. Consider Romans 5:1-5. What foundation do we have for building a close

   relationship with God? _____

   _____

7. Read Ephesians 1:1-14 and list several things that you have "in Christ."

Verse _____ _____

Verse _____ _____

Verse _____ _____

Verse _____ _____

Which of these is most important to you? Why? _____

_____

_____

THE PROCESS OF GROWTH

8. In regard to the following passages, what observations do you have about the process of spiritual growth?

a. 1 Peter 2:2-3 _____

_____

_____

b. Hebrews 5:13-14 _____

_____

_____

9. Where do good works fit into the Christian life (Ephesians 2:8-10)?

_____

_____

As you reflect on your life, you can be thankful for all that God is doing in you. Take a moment to express your gratitude to God for what He has done, is doing, and will do for you. Our outer person is merely God's frame; the real picture is the inner person who God, the Artist, is still creating.

THE MATURE LIFE

10. Who or what is the Christian's ultimate example (Ephesians 5:1-2)?

_____

_____

In what ways do you think a Christian can and should imitate Christ's lifestyle? _____

_____

_____

_____

11. What attitude should a mature Christian possess (Philippians 3:13-15)?

_____

_____

12. What are some character traits of a mature Christian (2 Peter 1:5-7)?

_____

_____

_____

Describe a person without these traits (2 Peter 1:8-11)? _____

_____

_____

_____

13. What stands out to you most from this Bible study? _____

_____

_____

_____

_____

_____

SUMMARY

Moving Toward Maturity

God intends for Christians to mature and become like Jesus Christ. God has saved Christians from the penalty of sin. They are now engaged in a conflict with sin but can anticipate a future with Christ, completely free from sin.

Your Starting Point

Faith in Jesus Christ marks the beginning of Christian growth (2 Corinthians 5:17). All believers have God's resources available to them to help them grow.

The Process of Growth

Spiritual growth is similar to physical growth. It takes time as God works in the believer's life.

The Mature Life

Growing in Christ is similar to walking. Following Christ's example and led by the Spirit, Christians are to walk in fellowship with Christ in faith and love. A mature Christian is one who continues to follow Christ, abounding in His work and experiencing His grace and love.

ASSIGNMENT FOR SESSION 3

1. Scripture Memory: Study and complete "Scripture Memory Guide—Week 3" (pages 25–26). Memorize the verse(s) on "Obedience to Christ": Romans 12:1 and John 14:21 (recommended but optional).
2. Quiet Time: Continue using *My Reading Highlights*, *My Reading Progress*, and a prayer sheet.
3. Bible Study: Complete the Bible study "Spiritual Warfare" (pages 33–36).
4. Other: Read and mark the article on "Relationship Evangelism" (pages 26–33) and come prepared to discuss it.

SESSION 3

OUTLINE OF THIS SESSION

1. Open the session in prayer.
2. Break into verse review groups and quote the verse(s) on "Obedience to Christ": Romans 12:1 and John 14:21 (recommended but optional). Work at getting everything signed that you can on *My Completion Record*.
3. Quote the verses learned in book 1.
4. Share quiet-time thoughts.
5. Discuss your observations from "Relationship Evangelism" (pages 26–33).
6. Discuss the Bible study "Spiritual Warfare" (pages 33–36).
7. Read "Assignment for Session 4" (page 37).
8. Close in prayer.

SCRIPTURE MEMORY GUIDE — WEEK 3

About the Verses

TOPIC 2: OBEDIENCE TO CHRIST
Jesus inseparably links His lordship to our obedience: "Why do you call me, 'Lord, Lord,' and do not do what I say?" (Luke 6:46). By obeying His will in day-to-day living, we acknowledge His leadership in our lives.

Romans 12:1 — This verse urges us to submit to Christ's lordship by yielding control of ourselves to Him. Because He has purchased us with the price of His own blood, this is the only reasonable thing to do. As we yield to Him and obey Him, we discover that His will for us is in every way "good, pleasing and perfect" (12:2).

John 14:21 (recommended but optional) — Jesus said that obedience to His Word is the proof of our love for Him: "Whoever has my commands and keeps them . . . loves me." But before we can keep His commands, we must have them — that is, we must know what He says to us in His Word. You will find that the verses you memorize this week will lead to stronger obedience to God.

Your Weekly Plan

1. Have a card for each verse you plan to memorize this week.

2. Start memorizing Romans 12:1, quoting the topic and reference and then adding one phrase at a time until you can quote the whole verse.

3. Plan to regularly quote aloud your memory verses from book 1 and your new book 2 verses.

4. You will find it helpful to manage your memorizing as you did in week 2. Each of these two patterns can be used no matter what day of the week your group meets:

- **Two-verse pattern**: If your 2:7 group meets on Sunday, plan to have the first verse memorized by Tuesday evening and continue to review it. Then you want to have the second verse memorized by Thursday evening and continue to review it as well. This gives you two full days to memorize each of the two verses and then three more days to review them both before you meet again on Sunday.

- **One-verse pattern**: If your 2:7 group meets on Sunday, plan to have your one verse memorized by Wednesday evening, and at the latest Thursday evening. Then review it at least once a day but preferably several times each day for the three or four days before your next group meeting.

5. You will find it extremely helpful to carry your memory cards with you, using spare moments for memorizing, reviewing, or meditating on these valuable verses.

6. Before going to your next 2:7 group meeting, you may want to write out your new verse or verses or quote them to someone before the day of your class. A trial run is always a good idea.

RELATIONSHIP EVANGELISM

Would you agree that most Christians are apprehensive about sharing their faith with others? While most Christians feel a responsibility to share Christ with the lost, many do not do so because of fear, lack of know-how, or uneasiness in using canned, unnatural approaches to sharing. Can you identify with any of the following excuses?

- **Not my gift**. "I really don't have the gift for evangelism. I leave that to people who like to confront other people."

- **Too nervous**. "I'm basically very shy. I choke up and my hands get sweaty when I have to talk to people about, you know, God. I'm sure God isn't calling me to share my faith."

- **I just don't know enough**. "I'm not a good Bible student. I just can't quote all those verses to convince people about God. Plus, I couldn't possibly answer all the questions they would have."

- **It's not my personality.** "I think you have to be the type that really loves people and is super-outgoing. That's just not for me."

Many Christians have overcome these excuses and discovered the joy and fruit that result from sharing their faith in Christ in the context of normal relationships with people. When there is mutual trust and respect in a relationship, the believer can easily and very effectively share his or her faith. Not very many Christians will volunteer for door-to-door or "cold-turkey" approaches to evangelism, but relationship evangelism is an approach in which everyone can be involved.

In his excellent book *Evangelism as a Lifestyle*,[1] Jim Petersen explores this approach to evangelism. Most of the material in quotes throughout this session is paraphrased or directly quoted from Petersen's book.

The Unreached World

"A large segment of the world's population is 'people not operating within a religious framework.' Religion is not a vital part of their existence. Their personal philosophy of life is not based on religious concepts. If asked about religion, they may give the 'right' answers. But they do not base their life or actions on any of those religious concepts.

"Others are totally ignorant of religious matters, even of the existence of religion. It may be difficult for most of us to imagine this, but there are population segments even in America where this is true.

"How much of the American population could be considered secularized? Recently, a *Christianity Today* Gallup Poll of Americans over 18 found that ninety-four percent believed in God or a universal spirit who functions in their mind as God. One-half of these said this belief gave them great comfort. About one-fourth believed that Jesus is fully God and fully man. Forty-five percent said personal faith in Christ is the only hope of heaven."[2]

How do we interpret these survey results? They obviously reflect a wide scattering of the gospel message. But what about those who find little or no comfort in the God they believe in? Apparently their position is simply a belief in a God who perhaps created the world and then withdrew. They don't think of Him as One who is actively involved in the everyday lives of men and women.

"The theologian Reinhold Niebuhr warned us to 'take no satisfaction in the prevailing religiosity of our nation. Much of it is a perversion of the Christian gospel.' ... In view of Gallup's statistics ... and our definition of the word *secular*, is it not reasonable to regard half of the American population as secularized—as people not operating within a religious framework?"

Our limited success in communicating across the frontiers of different mentalities and cultures indicates that we must be overlooking some major scriptural truths in this matter of communicating the gospel to the world. Have we limited our understanding of evangelism such that we are not really communicating to the secularized?

Proclaiming and Affirming the Gospel

In order to effectively communicate the gospel, we must first understand what the Scriptures teach about evangelism. The Scriptures speak of two primary means of evangelism:

1. The *proclamation* of the gospel: An *action* through which the non-Christian receives a clear statement of the essential message.
2. The *affirmation* of the gospel: A *process* of modeling and explaining the Christian message.

Both proclamation and affirmation are essential if we are to evangelize those from secular backgrounds as well as those who have religious backgrounds. One cannot be judged better or more effective than the other. Both are essential, and both are limited. The New Testament pattern seems to be that they should work together.

Proclaiming the Gospel

Proclamation "is an action through which the non-Christian receives a clear statement of the gospel message. It is something that happens at a certain point in time—for example, at church or during an evangelistic crusade, a radio or television broadcast, or a personal presentation of the gospel message to an individual. When someone declares the terms of a person's reconciliation to God, the gospel has been proclaimed."

The Bible commands us to proclaim the gospel to the entire world, so whether we should engage in this is beyond discussion. Proclamation, however, must be used wisely if we expect to communicate the message to all kinds of people. It is effective mainly among prepared people— that is, those who have a religious heritage. Proclamation, which focuses on reaping, is most effective where sowing and watering have taken place beforehand.

Proclaiming the gospel worked well for the first missionaries in the book of Acts: "They followed a certain tactic everywhere they went. First, they visited the synagogue. Obviously, almost everyone found in a synagogue would have some spiritual interest. Although these people had not heard about Christ, they were seeking after God according to their traditional patterns. They had the benefit of a religious heritage. The result was that many of them believed when Paul and Barnabas proclaimed the gospel."

Affirming the Gospel

The affirmation of the gospel is a *process* of demonstrating the Christian message. Affirmation is carried out by modeling a Christian lifestyle. This Christian lifestyle represents new values and attitudes to the non-Christian in the context of relationships. An example of a person affirming the gospel is the hardworking Christian who is unfairly passed over in a promotion and is able to graciously accept his or her circumstance. Demonstrating the Christian message by positive example is particularly effective among people without a Christian heritage and who do not believe that Christianity is a credible basis for their lives.

Steve, a businessman, fits into this category of secularized people. As a child, he had only limited church exposure and could not recall ever reading the Bible or talking about God at home. By the time he was twenty, religion had no part in Steve's thinking.

In his early twenties, Steve met and developed a friendship with Randy. They spent much time together going to movies, sporting events, and backpacking in the mountains. Randy was a Christian, but Steve noticed that he was not like other religious people he had met. Randy accepted him the way he was and did not criticize his lifestyle.

Randy asked Steve to attend church with him, and he did so on occasion. Usually Steve made fun of the sermons, but instead of becoming defensive, Randy would find some humor in Steve's remarks and laugh along with him. Unknown to Steve, Randy faithfully prayed for his salvation.

Five years after Steve and Randy met, Steve faced an emotional crisis. In despair, he considered ending his life but first turned to his one true friend for help. Steve poured out his heart to Randy. Randy listened carefully and then responded gently with the message of Jesus Christ, explaining how Christ could meet all of Steve's needs. That night, driving home, Steve opened his heart to the Savior.

Steve had not responded positively to a presentation of the gospel message previously. But Steve was observing Randy's life and was prayed for regularly. When Steve faced a crisis, he was then open to the proclamation of the gospel.

Evangelism as a Process

"When we bring someone to a decision to trust in Christ in the course of a conversation or two, we can be sure of one thing: Considerable preparation and laboring has already occurred in that life before we arrived on the scene. This is what Jesus was saying to the Twelve in John 4:36-38: 'The one who reaps draws a wage and harvests a crop for eternal life, so that the sower and the reaper may be glad together. Thus the saying "One sows and another reaps" is true. I sent you to reap what you have not worked for. Others have done the hard work, and you have reaped the benefits of their labor.'

"God uses many influences to prepare a person's heart for the gospel message: people, circumstances, and events.

"Some of the essential steps along the way only God can accomplish. The God-consciousness planted in the heart of every person is one of these (Romans 1:20). God has also written His law in people's hearts, accompanying it with a conscience and sense of guilt (Romans 2:14-15)."

Sometimes God uses job problems, broken relationships, uprooted homes, or personal tragedies that disrupt the routines and values of normal life. All of these events can serve to draw people away from the dominion of darkness and toward the kingdom of light.

"Even chance comments can be significant. An ex-Buddhist, describing his conversion to Christ, pointed back to a comment by his mother while they were in the Buddhist temple as being the trigger that started his search that led him to Christ. She wondered aloud why the 'true God' was positioned last, not first, on the shelf of idols in the temple. He never forgot his mother's question. Her comment prepared him to respond to the Christian gospel.

"God uses an endless variety of ways and means to sow the seed of the gospel message and move us along from ignorance and rebellion toward faith. The most obvious means, and by far the most effective, is a strong Christian family—growing up where the fundamentals of Christianity are practiced and taught in the home and church. After such an education, often the sole remaining need is reaping. People with a religious heritage still exist in significant numbers in many places. In these situations, reaping by itself produces encouraging results. This can lead us into thinking the whole world is at the same level of preparedness. It can make us forget that evangelism is, in fact, a process."

We must not be too anxious for the harvest, but we must keep in mind that before reaping come sowing, watering, and cultivating. Evangelism is not an event but a process. This process may take months and even years.

Attitudes for Success

What attitudes are necessary to effectively affirm the gospel to non-Christians?

1. We must be willing to initiate relationships.
2. We must show the same kind of love and acceptance toward sinners that Jesus displayed.

3. We must be willing to boldly identify with Christ early in a relationship.
4. We must demonstrate dependence on God through persevering prayer.

1. Initiate relationships. Let us look first at the area of taking initiative in relationships. In Matthew 5:43-48, Jesus taught that we should be like our Father, who causes the sun to rise on the evil and on the good. He continues in verses 46-48, "If you love those who love you, what reward will you get? Are not even the tax collectors doing that? And if you greet only your own people, what are you doing more than others? Do not even pagans do that? Be perfect, therefore, as your heavenly Father is perfect."

In developing relationships with non-Christians, we need to seek rapport. "Look for the common ground. Rapport occurs when two people share common interests and/or needs. This will cost us time and privacy, but how will others see God's grace in us if we keep our distance?

"In Luke 14:12-13, Jesus suggests that when we give a dinner we shouldn't invite just our friends and relatives. You know how that goes. This time it's our turn, next time it's theirs. In the end, everyone breaks even. It hasn't cost anyone anything. Rather, He says, invite the poor, the crippled, the lame, and the blind who cannot repay you—until the day of resurrection when they will be there

to salute your faithfulness to them.

"In other words, be hospitable. Deliberately break out of your daily routine of people and places for the gospel's sake."

There is perhaps no more effective environment for initiating evangelism than a dinner at home or a quiet restaurant. We must go into the world to establish the rapport needed to draw people into our lives.

2. Show acceptance and love. Our attitude must be one of acceptance and love. Jesus was the friend of publicans and sinners. We must accept people as they are. Be realistic about unbelievers and don't expect too much. They are not Christians, and they will probably act accordingly. Don't come across as a reformer.

The Christian tends to measure the non-Christian against a rather legalistic list of acceptable and unacceptable behavior. The list is a mixture of clear-cut commands from the Word of God, such as "Do not commit adultery," to standards that come from our traditions, such as total abstinence from alcohol.

"The non-Christian picks up the vibrations and feels he is being judged. He sometimes apologizes for his unacceptable habits, indicating that he feels he has fallen into the hands of someone bent on reforming him. Where there are such judgments, communication is hopeless.

"Acceptance does not mean approval. The contrast between our values and theirs will become conspicuous. Be sure this contrast is based on moral and scriptural matters, not on trivial and optional things. It is our responsibility to adapt to them unless absolute moral issues are involved. Make them feel comfortable around you. Be 'all things to all people' (1 Corinthians 9:22). Remember that sanctification is a matter of the heart, not surroundings.

"Avoid judging, preaching, condemning, or moralizing. 'No thank you' is definitely preferable to 'I don't smoke because I am a Christian and the Bible says . . .' Prayer before lunch that embarrasses your guest is not necessarily a good testimony! Demonstrate grace, not legalism. Be sensitive as to how your actions will affect the other person.

"Love people as they are and as individuals, not as targets for evangelism. Love. Accept. Adapt. Be a friend. . . . It has been said, 'Ninety percent of evangelism is love.'

"God's love for men and women is unconditional. His love is expressed through us as we commit ourselves to seeking the good of another, regardless of his or her response to us (1 John 3:16-18). There is an obvious link between loving and serving. If you answer the question, 'In what way can I serve this person?' you will have answered, 'How can I love this person?'"

3. Be bold. The next attitude that is necessary for the effective affirmation of the gospel is one of boldness—to be identified with Christ early in the relationship. We need to identify ourselves as Christians in the early stages because the longer we wait without saying anything, the harder witnessing will be at a later time. If we are to be honest in relating to our non-Christian friends, it is not wise to conceal our identity as Christians. We must be open about our relationship with Christ, yet we need to guard an overly aggressive spirit that would be threatening or offensive.

One way to "run up the flag" early in the relationship is to casually interject part of your spiritual story when the opportunity arises. As you pray for your friend, ask God to provide the opportunity to reveal your identity as a Christian in a positive, nonthreatening way. If you do this, you will experience a more relaxed relationship because you have been honest with your friend about who you really are. Identifying with Christ early in the relationship will also allow you to talk about spiritual things more easily later on.

4. Depend upon God through prayer. Finally, we must display an attitude of dependence upon God in prayer. We need to remember that the battle for souls is not a physical battle but a spiritual battle. Without wielding the weapon of prayer, we cannot expect to see God's deliverance. Not only does God want us to initiate and develop relationships, He wants us to pray faithfully for these people. "Pray your way through every step of the process, from establishing the first rapport, to opening the door to the message, to the Holy Spirit's convicting them of sin, righteousness, and judgment.

"Persist in prayer (Luke 11:9-10). George Mueller wrote, 'The great point is to never give up until that answer comes. I have been praying every day for 52 years for two men, sons of a friend of my youth. They are not converted yet, but they will be. . . . The great fault of the children of God is that they do not persevere. If they desire anything for God's glory, they should pray until they get it.' One of these men became a Christian at George Mueller's

funeral, the other some years later."

Proper attitudes are essential as we seek to affirm the gospel. First, willingness to initiate relationships will prevent us from isolating ourselves from the non-Christian world. Then, displaying love and acceptance toward sinners will enable us to manifest the grace of God and avoid the common pitfall of a legalistic and judgmental spirit. Next, boldly identifying with Christ early in the relationship will allow us to relate honestly with our non-Christian friends and make it easier for us to discuss spiritual things later on. Finally, a commitment to depend on God will stimulate us to persist in daily prayer for those non-Christian friends God has given us.

SPIRITUAL WARFARE

To discover and apply the great truth of God's Word is to enter the field of spiritual warfare. A battle rages for the hearts and minds of men and women. But growth comes with conflict, and God has promised that "in all these things we are more than conquerors through him who loved us" (Romans 8:37).

> **THINK ABOUT:**
>
> What elements in military conflict also exist in spiritual warfare?

THE BATTLE

1. Read 2 Timothy 2:3-4. How would you describe the kind of life Paul wrote about? _____

_____

_____

2. How is the Christian life described by the apostle Paul in Ephesians 6:12?

_____

_____

_____

3. How did Satan discredit God's Word when he deceived Eve (Genesis 3:1-5)?

_____

_____

_____

Satan makes it his continual business to cast doubt on God's Word and to discredit God's Son.

4. What can be learned about our Enemy, Satan, in the following verses?

Luke 8:12 _____

_____

_____

John 8:44 _____

_____

_____

2 Corinthians 4:3-4 _____

_____

_____

2 Corinthians 11:3 _____

_____

2 Corinthians 11:14 _____

_____

_____

5. Read the account of Christ's confrontation with Satan (the Devil) in Luke 4:1-13.

a. What was Jesus' condition when the Devil appeared? _____

_____

_____

b. To what desires did the Devil appeal in the three temptations?

_____

_____

THE OPPOSITION

We receive opposition from three sources: the world, the flesh, and the Devil.

6. From the following passages, what characterizes the world, the flesh, and the Devil?

John 15:18-19   James 4:1-3   1 Peter 5:8-9
Ephesians 2:3   John 8:44   Colossians 2:8

The World

Verse(s) _____ _____

Verse(s) _____ _____

The Flesh

Verse(s) _____ _____

Verse(s) _____ _____

The Devil

Verse(s) _____ _____

Verse(s) _____ _____

VICTORY HAS BEEN PROVIDED

Over the World

7. According to the following passages, what is the basis for victory over the world?

a. 1 John 5:4-5 _____

b. John 17:14-18 _____

c. Colossians 2:6-8 _____

Over the Flesh

8. From the following passages, how can we have victory over the flesh?

a. Ephesians 4:22-24 _____

_____

b. Galatians 5:16-17 _____

_____

c. Romans 6:12-13 _____

_____

> Let no man think that he can have any measure of victory over
> his inner corruption without taking it to the Lord again and
> again in prayer.
>
> —GEORGE MUELLER

Over the Devil

9. According to Hebrews 2:14-15, what did Christ's death on the cross mean

   for Satan? _____

   _____

   _____

   What does it mean for us today? _____

   _____

10. Please write out 1 Corinthians 15:57 in your own words as a personal
    prayer. Take a moment to thank God for your assurance of daily victory

    in Jesus Christ. _____

    _____

    _____

    _____

SUMMARY

The Battle

All Christians are involved in a spiritual battle between God and the forces of
evil. Satan is the major adversary of God and people.

The Opposition

The Christian has three very real enemies in the spiritual battle: the world, the
flesh, and the Devil.

The Victory Has Been Provided

The battle has already been won in Christ. Victory over the world, the flesh,
and the Devil becomes possible through Christ and His new life in us.

ASSIGNMENT FOR SESSION 4

1. Scripture Memory: Study and complete "Scripture Memory Guide—Week 4" (pages 39–40). Memorize the verse(s) on "The Word": 2 Timothy 3:16 and Joshua 1:8 (recommended but optional).

2. Quiet Time: Continue reading, marking, responding back to God in prayer, recording on *My Reading Highlights*, and using a prayer sheet.

3. Bible Study: Complete the Bible study "Faith and the Truths of God" (pages 40–44).

4. Other: Please bring your prayer sheets to class.

SESSION 4

OUTLINE OF THIS SESSION

1. Open the session in prayer.
2. Break into verse review groups and quote the verse(s) on "The Word": 2 Timothy 3:16 and Joshua 1:8 (recommended but optional).
3. Share quiet-time thoughts from *My Reading Highlights.*
4. Share results from using your prayer sheets.
5. Discuss the Bible study "Faith and the Truths of God" (pages 40–44).
6. Read "Assignment for Session 5" (page 44).
7. Have a period of conversational prayer.

SCRIPTURE MEMORY GUIDE—WEEK 4

About the Verses

TOPIC 3: THE WORD

The Bible in a practical sense is the foundation of the Christian life, since all we know about Jesus Christ, the true Foundation, we learn from the Bible.

2 Timothy 3:16—This verse tells us that all Scripture is inspired by God (literally, God-breathed). Peter put it this way: "Prophets, though human, spoke from God as they were carried along by the Holy Spirit" (2 Peter 1:21). The Scriptures are given to teach, reprove, correct, and train us in righteous living. God did not give us His Word primarily to increase our knowledge but rather to transform our lives.

Joshua 1:8 (recommended but optional)—This verse promises that those who do what God's Word says will prosper. The first step to applying His Word is to meditate on it frequently, mulling it over in our minds. Thoughtfully reviewing previously memorized verses is a great way to meditate on Scripture.

Your Weekly Plan

1. For each verse you plan to memorize this week, have a card with the topic, reference, verse, and reference on one side and only the topic and reference on the other side.

2. Start memorizing 2 Timothy 3:16, quoting the topic and reference and then adding one phrase at a time until you can quote the whole verse. When you are memorizing two verses in one week, you want to memorize the first verse in two days, then the second verse in two days, leaving three days to sharpen them both through review (more than

once a day if possible).

3. Each day quote aloud the verses you memorized in book 1 along with the verses you have learned in book 2.

4. Plan to carry your verse cards with you so you can use spare moments during the day to memorize, review, or meditate on your verses.

5. Before meeting with your group for session 4, write out your new verse(s) from memory or quote your verse(s) to someone just to check accuracy.

FAITH AND THE TRUTHS OF GOD

A group of people once asked Jesus how they could do the work of God. Jesus replied, "The work of God is this: to believe in the one he has sent" (John 6:29). God desires belief and faith from individuals, for "without faith it is impossible to please God" (Hebrews 11:6).

But often in modern society, faith is nothing more than wishful thinking: "I hope everything works out all right. I have 'faith' that it will." The biblical concept of faith far surpasses this superficial approach and is an important ingredient in walking with Christ.

THINK ABOUT:

What do you think the following illustration is attempting to communicate?

WALKING BY FAITH

1. From the following verses, how would you define faith?

   Acts 27:25 _____

   _____

   Romans 4:20-21 _____

   _____

   Hebrews 11:1 _____

   _____

   > Faith is the assurance that the thing that God has said in His
   > Word is true and that God will act according to what He has
   > said in His Word. . . . Faith is not a matter of impressions, nor of
   > probabilities, nor of appearances.
   >
   > —GEORGE MUELLER

The opposite of faith in the living God is not doubt; it is unbelief. Doubt only
needs more facts. Unbelief is disobedience: refusing to acknowledge and follow God's truth.

OBJECTS OF FAITH

2. To the right of each Scripture reference, note some unworthy objects in
   which people place their faith. Then place an "X" by those on which you
   find yourself more likely to depend.

   _____ Psalm 1:1 _____

   _____ Psalm 33:16-17 _____

   _____ Proverbs 3:5 _____

   _____ Jeremiah 9:23-24 _____

   What do you feel is the inevitable result of placing faith in these objects?

   _____

   _____

   _____

   _____

   _____

   _____

3. God makes and fulfills promises. What do the following passages teach about God?

1 Kings 8:56 _____

_____

Psalm 89:34 _____

_____

2 Peter 1:4 _____

_____

Numbers 23:19 _____

_____

> Faith always attached itself to what God has said or promised.
> When an honorable man says anything, he also does it; on the
> back of the saying follows the doing. So also is it with God:
> When He would do anything, He says so first through His Word.
> —ANDREW MURRAY

EXAMPLES OF FAITH

4. As you read Hebrews 11, please list at least three things that strike you about the passage.

_____

_____

_____

_____

_____

TRUTHS YOU CAN TRUST

5. Please fill in the following chart.

VERSE	TRUTH	CONDITION, IF ANY
John 15:7		
Isaiah 26:3		

Romans 8:28-29 _____ _____

_____ _____

How to handle the Bible:

- get everything out of it,
- do not read anything into it,
- let nothing remain unread in it.

—J. A. BENGEL

6. Why do you feel that God places conditions on some promises?

_____

_____

What should our attitude be toward God's promises (Hebrews 6:12)?

_____

_____

_____

It is helpful and encouraging to note God's promises. You may want to keep a list of these promises, their conditions, and their results. God's promises often form a "chain" as in the following example.

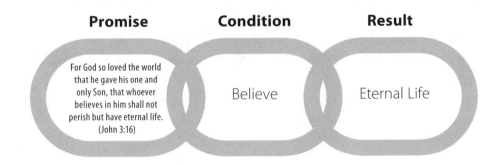

Promise   **Condition**   **Result**

For God so loved the world that he gave his one and only Son, that whoever believes in him shall not perish but have eternal life. (John 3:16)   Believe   Eternal Life

7. What is one promise you have discovered in your Bible reading? _____

_____

_____

Specifically, how has this promise helped you? _____

_____

_____

SUMMARY

Walking by Faith

Faith is based on the certain Word of God. Believing God and His Word gives the Christian the experience of hope, joy, peace, answered prayer, and the fulfillment of many other promises of God.

Objects of Faith

People may entrust their lives to a number of things that will ultimately fail. Only God and His Word are worthy of our complete trust.

Examples of Faith

Many men and women throughout history have believed God and trusted Him. Hebrews 11 is a Hall of Fame list of some of those people.

Truths You Can Trust

Promises often have conditions; this is true of God's promises. We must not be careless or presumptuous in handling His Word.

ASSIGNMENT FOR SESSION 5

1. Scripture Memory: Study and complete "Scripture Memory Guide—Week 5" (pages 45–46).
   a. Memorize the verse(s) on "Prayer": John 15:7 and Philippians 4:6-7 (recommended but optional).
   b. Please take the Self-Checking Quiz on pages 46–47.
2. Quiet Time: Continue reading, marking, responding, recording, and using your prayer sheets.
3. Bible Study: Complete the Bible study "Knowing God's Will" (pages 48–52).

SESSION 5

OUTLINE OF THIS SESSION

1. Open the session in prayer.
2. Break into verse review groups and quote the verse(s) on "Prayer": John 15:7 and Philippians 4:6-7 (recommended but optional). Work at getting everything signed that you can on *My Completion Record*.
3. Briefly discuss the Self-Checking Quiz on pages 46–47.
4. Share quiet-time thoughts from *My Reading Highlights*.
5. Discuss the Bible study "Knowing God's Will" (pages 48–52).
6. Read "Assignment for Session 6" (page 52).
7. Close in prayer. Focus on people from your evangelism prayer list.

SCRIPTURE MEMORY GUIDE—WEEK 5

About the Verses

TOPIC 4: PRAYER

Direct communication with our heavenly Father is one of the greatest privileges a child of God has. We are urged to come confidently to God in prayer, especially in time of need (Hebrews 4:16). God's antidote for worry is prayer. None of our concerns is too small or mundane to bring before God in prayer.

John 15:7—This verse presents two conditions for receiving what we ask for in prayer. First, we are abiding in Christ; that is, we maintain unbroken fellowship with Him. Second, we must allow His Word to abide in us, keeping it in our thoughts so it will direct our lives.

Philippians 4:6-7 (recommended but optional)—It is a specific kind of praying that God wants: prayer with thanksgiving. Learn to thank God for everything, difficulties as well as blessings. Prayer can replace anxiety with peace.

The late Dr. Ole Hallesby, Norwegian seminary professor, gives the following encouraging words in his book *Prayer*: "My helpless friend, your helplessness is the most powerful plea which rises up to the tender father-heart of God. He has heard your prayer from the very first that you honestly cried to him in your need, and night and day he inclines his ear toward earth in order to ascertain if any of the helpless children of men are turning to him in their distress.

"Be not anxious because of your helplessness. Above all, do not let it prevent you from praying. Helplessness is the real secret and the impelling power of prayer."[3]

Your Weekly Plan

1. For each verse you plan to memorize this week, have a card with the topic, reference, verse, and reference on one side and only the topic and reference on the other side.

2. Start memorizing John 15:7, quoting the topic and reference and then adding one phrase at a time until you can quote the whole verse.

Continue to use the success pattern you have learned for memorizing two verses per week.

3. Each day quote aloud the verses you memorized in book 1 along with the verses you have learned in book 2.

4. Plan to carry your verse cards with you so you can use spare moments during the day to memorize, review, or meditate on your verses.

5. Take the Self-Checking Quiz (pages 46–47).

SELF-CHECKING QUIZ

You want to take this quiz after reviewing the Scripture memory guides for weeks 1 through 5. These are great reminders of proven approaches for memorizing Scripture. Correct answers appear at the end of the quiz on page 47.

1. Memorizing Scripture is nourishment for your soul and is like stocking the pantry of your heart for future needs.
   T **F** (Circle **T** for true and **F** for false)

2. Match the following. Write the number of the correct answer in the blank space before each statement to complete it.
   (1) helps you understand the verses in their setting and makes them more meaningful and easier to remember and use.
   (2) makes it possible for you to use spare moments for memorizing, reviewing, and meditating.
   (3) gives you the big picture and shows you where you are going in Scripture memory.
   (4) helps you progress step-by-step in your memory work and avoid pitfalls.
   (5) hinders your ability to recall the verse later.
   (6) helps you remember where the verses are located in the Bible.
   (7) helps you speed the learning process.
   (8) should be placed inside your verse pack.
   _____ a. It is important to carefully follow the "Your Weekly Plan" section because it . . .
   _____ b. Reading the "About the Verses" comments and

looking up the context in your Bible . . .

_____ c. The verses you have already learned . . .

_____ d. The principle of saying the reference before and after the verse . . .

_____ e. Becoming familiar with the topical outline of the course before learning the verses . . .

_____ f. Working on a verse multiple times during the day . . .

_____ g. Carrying your verse pack with you at all times . . .

_____ h. When reviewing, you should not glance at the first words of the verse because this . . .

3. Why is it important that you have clearly in mind your own reasons for memorizing Scripture? (Check the correct answer.)

_____ a. So you can check them off when these goals have been reached

_____ b. So you will take pride in your memory work

_____ c. So these reasons will motivate you and help you succeed

4. It is best to learn the verses word perfect because this . . . (Check three correct answers.)

_____ a. teaches you to observe details.

_____ b. makes a clear impression on your mind so that the verses are easier to recall.

_____ c. enables you to use them accurately.

_____ d. impresses others with your knowledge of Scripture.

_____ e. gives you confidence in using your verses.

5. Why is it recommended that you learn only one or two verses a week? (Check three correct answers.)

_____ a. To give you ample opportunity to look up the context of the verses

_____ b. To keep you from getting through the course too quickly

_____ c. To give you time to meditate on the verses and apply them to your life

_____ d. To help you develop good memory habits and succeed in Scripture memory

_____ e. To give you the scientifically proven optimum rate of learning

6. An excellent way to get an early start on your daily memory work is to include it as part of your morning quiet time.
   T   F

7. The verses in "Live the New Life" deal with the essential elements of the obedient, Christ-centered life.
   T   F

Correct answers:

1-T; 2 a-4, b-1, c-8, d-6, e-3, f-7, g-2, h-5; 3-c; 4-a,b,c; 5-a,c,d; 6-T; 7-T

KNOWING GOD'S WILL

Christians often wonder what God wants them to do concerning their desires and plans. Often it seems that God's will is hidden in a buried treasure chest and that we have only small portions of the map to find its location. But is this true? Is God keeping His plans hidden and secret, or is He interested in having you follow Him so that He can lead you step-by-step?

A passage of Scripture that deals with this issue is Proverbs 3:5-6, which you memorized in book 1. Can you quote that passage right now? Please check the box after you quote it. ☐

| **THINK ABOUT:** |
| To what extent can someone else determine God's will for your life? |

GOD'S WILL

1. What should be our goals as followers of Christ (Ephesians 5:15-17)?

   _____

   _____

   _____

2. What would God like to do for us (Psalm 32:8)? _____

   _____

   _____

3. What is the Holy Spirit's role (Romans 8:14)? _____

   _____

> The will of God is not like a magic package let down out of heaven by a string. . . . The will of God is like a scroll that unrolls every day. . . . God will guide you and me. . . one day at a time. . . . Our call then is to follow the Lord Jesus Christ . . . in a daily close relationship. It is first of all *being*, not *doing*. . . . As we realize this, we will begin to sense the exhilaration each day can hold when we are living hand in hand with God, the Holy Spirit guiding us, unrolling the scroll.
>
> —PAUL LITTLE

In the Scriptures, Christians have all the guidance they need in order to live for Jesus Christ. However, there are certain specific decisions that must be made even though the Bible does not give specific instructions. In these cases, a Christian wants to apply scriptural principles.

GUIDANCE PRINCIPLES

God has given biblical directives to guide us in how we live our lives. If we are considering a course of action inconsistent with God's Word, then we know that it is not His will for us.

4. Using the following verses, state in your own words some of God's objectives for every Christian.

    God wants us to . . .

    Matthew 6:33 _____

    Matthew 22:37-39 _____

    Matthew 28:18-20 _____

    _____

    1 Thessalonians 5:18 _____

    2 Timothy 2:2 _____

    1 Peter 1:15 _____

    2 Peter 3:18 _____

    Ask yourself the following questions based on these and similar verses to determine your course of action:

    a. Am I putting God's desire ahead of my own?

    b. Will my course of action help me love God and others more?

    c. How does this action relate to my personal involvement in reaching and discipling people?

    d. Will it contribute to my leading a more holy life?

    e. Will it move me toward more Christian training and spiritual growth?

    f. Can I be thankful for whatever the results or however it works out?

5. Using the following verses from 1 Corinthians, develop questions that could help a person discern God's will.

    6:12 _____

    6:19-20 _____

    8:9 _____

10:31 _____

OBEDIENCE TO GOD

If we refuse to follow what God has already shown us, won't He be less likely to give us further direction? Obeying God's known will influences the degree to which we receive further guidance from God.

6. What other action can we take to learn God's will?

   Psalm 143:8 _____

   James 1:5 _____

7. What conditions are given in Romans 12:1-2 for finding God's will?

   _____

   _____

   _____

8. Read Psalm 27:14 and Isaiah 30:18. How does "waiting on the Lord"

   relate to knowing God's will? How do you do it? _____

   _____

   _____

   _____

   _____

> Satan rushes people—God guides them.
>
> —UNKNOWN

OPENNESS TO GOD'S LEADING

Many difficulties in determining the Lord's will are overcome when you are ready to do His will, whatever it may be.

9. You may not always know all of the possible alternatives in determining what to do. According to Proverbs 15:22, what is a means by which you

   can gather additional information? _____

   _____

   _____

10. Read Psalm 1:1.

    a. Of what counsel should we be skeptical? _____

    _____

b. When is it valid to seek a non-Christian's advice? _____

_____

_____

11. What are some other considerations that can help you discern God's leading? Match the following verses with the appropriate factors.

_____ Careful and wise thinking   a. 2 Corinthians 2:12-13

_____ Inner spiritual peace   b. Philippians 1:12-14

_____ Particular circumstances   c. Ephesians 5:15-17

What possible dangers exist in relying on only these factors? _____

_____

_____

_____

PRINCIPLES IN PRACTICE

In questions 1–11 you identified several biblical principles for knowing God's will and following His leading. A good way to put those principles into practice is to approach a decision with a checklist of one-word principles. Ask yourself how that decision matches up with each of the six factors. Two need further explanation. Both are more subjective than the others.

1. Objectives	Questions 4–5
2. Obedience	Questions 6–8
3. Openness	Questions 9–11
4. Counsel	Questions 9–10
5. Peace	Question 11
6. Circumstances	Question 11

Peace: Do you feel uneasy about following one of your options, or do you sense an inner peace that "God is in this"?

Circumstances: Does a set of circumstances seem to support one of your options? Do those circumstances seem to be more than coincidence?

12. Some passages in the Bible illustrate elements that affect sound judgment. Study the following examples. What was the influencing factor in making either the right or wrong decision?

PERSON	PASSAGE	INFLUENCING FACTOR
Gideon	Judges 6:36-38	
Moses	Hebrews 11:25-26	
Demas	2 Timothy 4:10	

SUMMARY

God's Will

God wants us to live productive, fulfilled lives. One reason He has given us the Scriptures is so we might know both His specific directives and broad principles for living.

Guidance Principles

If we are to walk in God's will, we need to pursue scriptural objectives and, with the Holy Spirit's help, continue to obey God's known will. We need to want what God wants.

Principles in Practice

When making relatively significant decisions, it is wise to use a checklist of factors that should be considered. These factors should include objectives, obedience, openness, counsel, peace, and circumstances.

ASSIGNMENT FOR SESSION 6

1. Scripture Memory: Study and complete "Scripture Memory Guide—Week 6" (pages 53–54). Memorize the verse(s) on "Fellowship": Hebrews 10:24-25 and 1 John 1:3 (recommended but optional).
2. Quiet Time: Continue reading, marking, responding back to God in prayer, recording on *My Reading Highlights*, and using a prayer sheet.
3. Bible Study: Complete the Bible study "Walking as a Servant" (pages 55–59).
4. Other: Work on getting everything signed that you can on *My Completion Record*.

SESSION 6

OUTLINE OF THIS SESSION

1. Open the session in prayer.
2. Break into verse review groups and quote the verse(s) on "Fellowship": Hebrews 10:24-25 and 1 John 1:3 (recommended but optional). Get some things signed on *My Completion Record*.
3. Share quiet-time thoughts from *My Reading Highlights*.
4. Read and discuss "Suggestions for Developing Friendships with Non-Christians" (pages 54–55).
5. Discuss the Bible study "Walking as a Servant" (pages 55–59).
6. Discuss a tentative time and place for session 8.
7. Read "Assignment for Session 7" (page 59).
8. Close in prayer. Pray about developing true friendships with non-Christians.

SCRIPTURE MEMORY GUIDE—WEEK 6

About the Verses
TOPIC 5: FELLOWSHIP

A strong follower of Christ will actively seek fellowship with other believers—individually, in small groups, and in a local church. As members of one body, we depend on one another. You are discovering in your 2:7 group the valuable contribution to your life that other believers can make. This is according to God's design: "Now you are the body of Christ, and each one of you is a part of it" (1 Corinthians 12:27); "You are . . . fellow citizens with God's people and also members of his household" (Ephesians 2:19).

Hebrews 10:24-25—This passage teaches that we should encourage one another to love and good works through regular fellowship. Our faith and obedience to Christ can be stimulated by fellowship with other believers, as can theirs by fellowship with us.

1 John 1:3 (recommended but optional)—This verse explains that true Christian fellowship is centered around Christ and is more than just socializing; God Himself is present when we meet together with other believers.

Your Weekly Plan

1. For each verse you plan to memorize this week, have a card with the topic, reference, verse, and reference

on one side and only the topic and reference on the other side.

2. Start memorizing Hebrews 10:24-25, quoting the topic and reference and then adding one phrase at a time until you can quote the whole verse. If you are memorizing two verses in one week, you want to continue the pattern of memorizing a new verse every two days.

3. Each day quote aloud the verses you memorized in book 1 along with your new book 2 verses.

4. Plan to carry your verse cards with you so you can use spare moments during the day to memorize, review, or meditate on your verses.

SUGGESTIONS FOR DEVELOPING FRIENDSHIPS WITH NON-CHRISTIANS

A part of your evangelism assignment in this course is to have an activity with someone who has not yet come to faith in Christ. The purpose of this activity is to start or deepen your friendship with that person. Of course, one activity does not establish a friendship, so pray for the person and ask others to pray. Perhaps be thinking of other things you might do with this person as part of a group or just you two. (To avoid complications, it is wise to seek out only people who are your gender.)

The ideas shared here are not intended to be manipulative or insincere. Men and women in other 2:7 groups have appreciated the practical suggestions mentioned here.

The activity you choose should be a natural thing that you can do together. It could be as simple as having a cup of coffee together. Here are a few suggestions:

- Play a sport together or attend a sports event.
- Help the person with a task or project.
- Discuss a hobby or participate together in a hobby.
- Attend a concert or theatrical performance.
- Work on a community project as volunteers.

The possibilities are almost endless, but some options will fit your situation better than others.

Jesus spent so much time with non-Christians that He was called "a friend of . . . sinners" (Matthew 11:19). He took the initiative to seek out those who needed Him. We can too.

Choose to be where they are. Be outside when neighbors are. Have a barbeque and invite some neighbors. Join a club. Initiate interesting conversations at coffee and lunch breaks. Talk about topics that interest them or are mutual interests. Smile—sincerely from the heart. Know their name and use it when you are with them. Avoid controversial topics until the friendship is quite well established.

You are praying about seeing some of your acquaintances become friends. This may take time. But evangelism is a process that can be done patiently and sincerely. You lay the foundation for a person's coming to faith in Christ, through you or others.

WALKING AS A SERVANT

Serving is one of the greatest challenges in the life of a disciple. Everyone enjoys being served, but few make an effort to serve others. People don't mind being called servants, but they don't want to be treated as servants. The mature Christian is marked by what he or she will do for others without expecting anything in return.

> **THINK ABOUT:**
>
> Jesus was the Creator of the universe, yet He was the supreme example of a servant. If He were a twenty-first-century man, how do you think He would demonstrate His servanthood?

CHRIST, YOUR EXAMPLE

1. What was Christ's purpose in coming to this world (Mark 10:45)?

   _____

2. Read John 13:1-17.
   a. How did Jesus serve the disciples? _____

   _____

   b. Why was Jesus able to give so freely of Himself (see verse 3)? _____

   _____

   c. List several lessons that stand out to you from Christ's example in this passage.

   _____

   _____

   _____

   _____

> The Son of God became the servant of God in order to fulfill the mission of God.
>
> —J. OSWALD SANDERS

3. How should we be like Christ (Philippians 2:5-8)? _____

_____

_____

4. According to the following verses, who were some of the people who gladly bore the title "servant"?

Exodus 14:31 _____

1 Samuel 1:11 _____

1 Samuel 3:9 _____

1 Samuel 29:8 _____

Luke 1:38 _____

1 Corinthians 4:1 _____

5. What perspective did Paul have about being a servant (1 Corinthians 4:1-5)? _____

_____

_____

_____

_____

CHRIST'S DESIRE FOR YOU

6. What qualifications determined who would serve (Acts 6:1-7)? _____

_____

_____

7. How does having an attitude of humility affect how we relate to others

(Philippians 2:3-4)? _____

_____

_____

_____

GIVING OF YOURSELF

8. What are some reasons why serving is difficult (Luke 22:24-27)?

_____

_____

_____

9. Read Galatians 5:13-15; 6:9-10.

   a. What can hold us back from serving others to our full capacity?

   _____

   _____

   _____

   b. What can motivate us to serve others in spite of hindrances?

   _____

   _____

   _____

   c. What is one hindrance to your serving others?

   _____

   _____

   _____

Christians have been set free in Christ—not to do whatever they please, but to serve. Believers have been:

- Set free from sin, to serve righteousness (Romans 6:18-19)
- Set free from Satan, to serve God (1 Peter 2:16)
- Set free from self, to serve others (Galatians 5:13)

Christians are no longer under obligation to serve the things of the old life; they are now free to voluntarily serve the things of the new life.

10. Who did Paul serve? Why?

   1 Corinthians 9:19 _____

   _____

   2 Corinthians 4:4-5 _____

   _____

11. Read Proverbs 3:27 and 1 John 3:17. What do these verses ask you to do?

_____

_____

_____

_____

With what common needs could you help another person or family?

_____

_____

_____

12. In what ways can you serve others?

Romans 14:19 _____

Ephesians 4:32 _____

1 Thessalonians 5:11 _____

James 5:16 _____

1 John 3:11 _____

13. As a servant, we could become proud of our serving. What are some guidelines to help us keep from becoming proud (Luke 17:7-10)?

_____

_____

_____

_____

SUMMARY

Christ, Your Example

Jesus Christ was not obligated to become a servant. He did so voluntarily. While on earth, Jesus served people in a variety of ways, giving of Himself to meet people's needs.

Christ's Desire for You

We want to be a person who, like Christ, serves others. When we have an attitude of humility, we are more able to serve well.

Giving of Yourself

We want to overcome hindrances to serving and be active in meeting some of the needs of others. There are many practical ways in which we can be caring servants.

ASSIGNMENT FOR SESSION 7

1. Scripture Memory: No new verse is assigned for next time. Continue to sharpen the verses you have learned. Review aloud whenever possible.
2. Quiet Time: Continue reading, marking, responding back to God in prayer, recording on *My Reading Highlights*, and using a prayer sheet.
3. My Story:
   a. Study the "My Story" information on pages 61–72.
   b. Fill out one of the three "My Story" worksheets on pages 72–76.
4. Other: Work on getting everything completed that you can on *My Completion Record*.

SESSION 7

OUTLINE OF THIS SESSION

1. Open the session in prayer.
2. Break into verse review groups and quote all the verses you have learned up to this point in book 2. Work at getting more items completed and signed on *My Completion Record*.
3. Read "Congratulations!" (page 61).
4. Discuss the material on "My Story" preparation (pages 61–72).
   a. "Why Prepare 'My Story'" (pages 61–62)
   b. "Preparing 'My Story' General Comments" (pages 62–63)
   c. "The Grape Illustration" (pages 63 and 64)
   d. "Effective 'My Story' Preparation" (pages 63–67)
   e. "Two Ways You Might Organize Your Story" (pages 67–68)
   f. "Choosing Your 'My Story' Format" (pages 68–72)
5. Read "The Session 8 Workshop" (pages 76–77).
6. Finalize the time and place for the session 8 workshop.
7. Discuss a tentative time and place for session 11, your Extended Time with God.
8. Read "Assignment for Session 8" (page 77).
9. Close in prayer. Focus on people from your evangelism prayer list and any upcoming friendship activity.

CONGRATULATIONS!

You are to be commended for your perseverance in completing book 1 and proceeding successfully to this point in book 2 in THE 2:7 SERIES. The Lord has helped you reach some difficult but meaningful milestones in your spiritual development. By God's grace, you will soon be a graduate of book 2, walking closer to God and being better prepared to serve Him wherever He wants to use you.

WHY PREPARE "MY STORY"

The apostle Peter challenges us, "Always be prepared to give an answer to everyone who asks you to give the reason for the hope that you have" (1 Peter

3:15). One of the most effective tools you have for sharing your faith is the story of how Jesus Christ gave you eternal life and how He has enriched your life. The apostle John wrote, "We proclaim to you what we have seen and heard" (1 John 1:3). John was testifying about his relationship with Jesus Christ.

When the apostle Paul stood before King Agrippa (Acts 26), he spoke simply, logically, and clearly about his life *before* salvation, *how* he met Christ, and what his life was like *after* conversion. Paul's story takes three or four minutes to read aloud in a conversational manner.

Although you will be writing "My Story," the purpose is not to memorize it and give it verbatim; it's to help you put into words some of the important and interesting details of your conversion. The choice of the right words, the flow of your story, and knowing how to begin and end are all important. As you begin to work on this, ask the Lord for wisdom and insight into just how to share your story. Be open to suggestions from your group leader.

Many graduates of THE 2:7 SERIES have said that the preparation done on "My Story" was one of the most beneficial parts of their discipleship training. Many people have come to Christ simply because others like you have sharpened their "story" while going through THE 2:7 SERIES. It is an effective way to prepare "to give an answer to everyone who asks you to give the reason for the hope that you have."

Trust God and work hard. You want to give time, thought, and prayer to this important part of your discipleship training.

PREPARING "MY STORY" GENERAL COMMENTS

You will be able to complete all or most of "My Story" by the end of a special workshop in session 8. During session 9, some time may be given for hearing each other's stories. Also, one or two in your group might need to complete their stories during session 9.

1. PRIMARY AIM
The primary aim is for you to complete and verbally tell your story from an outline on an index card.

2. NUMBER OF DRAFTS
The amount of time and effort it takes each person to prepare his or her story can vary greatly. This has little to do with intelligence or spirituality; it has everything to do with the complexity of some people's stories.

3. DIFFICULT BUT REWARDING

Many students find working on their salvation story to be the most profitable and stimulating part of this course; others face some discouragement while going through this process. Your attitude and how aggressively you do your work can make all the difference. Persevere! Pray for God's wisdom and guidance.

4. SALVATION STORY

Testimonials can be prepared on many subjects and tailored to various audiences. The salvation story we prepare during this course:

- Will be designed to give to a person who is not yet a Christian
- Will be best suited for sharing one to one or in a small group
- Will primarily serve as a "door opener," not a "convincing tool"

Many people are not ready to be convinced that they need Christ, but can often be open to talk about the gospel after an inoffensive telling of a salvation story.

THE GRAPE ILLUSTRATION

As we continue to mature in Christ and have more life experience, we accumulate stories on a number of life issues (see page 64). These become stories we can tell to encourage others and help them grow in Christ. "My Story"—your personal salvation story—helps move people toward faith in Christ.

EFFECTIVE "MY STORY" PREPARATION

OUTLINE FOR "MY STORY"

In Acts 22 and 26, Paul explains how he came to Christ. The two stories give us a biblical model that can help us write our own salvation stories. Here is Paul's outline in Acts 26:

Lead-In	Verses 2-3
BEFORE	Verses 4-11
HOW	Verses 12-20
AFTER	Verses 21-23
Close	Verses 24-29

During sessions 7 and 8, you are preparing your *before*, *how*, and *after*. In one of your group sessions, you will have the opportunity to tell your salvation

The Grape Illustration

Various types of testimonies one can
accumulate through Christian experience

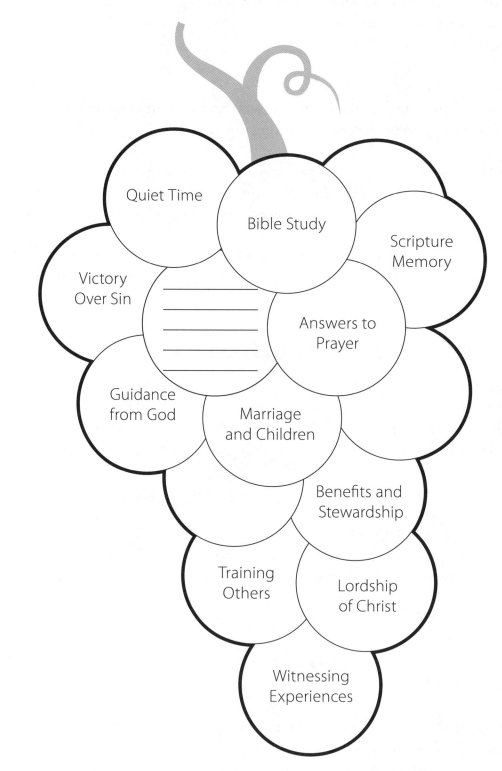

story in less than four minutes. In session 9, more will be said about the lead-in and close.

GUIDELINES FOR PREPARING THE MORE SPECIFIC CONTENT

1. *Make it sound conversational.* Avoid literary-sounding statements. Use informal language.
2. *Share; don't preach.* Say "I" and "me," not "you." This keeps your story warm and personal.
3. *Avoid religious words, phrases, and jargon.*

RELIGIOUS TERMS	POSSIBLE SUBSTITUTES
Believe/Accept Christ	Trusted or relied on Christ for my salvation
Sin	Rebelled against God's ways, hurt God by my actions
Went forward	Decided to turn my life over to God
Under the blood	God forgave the wrongs I had done
Saved/Born again	Accepted God's forgiveness
Christian	A follower of Christ, real Christian

4. *Generalize so more people can identify with your story.* It is better to not name specific churches, denominations, or groups. Avoid using dates and ages.
5. *Include some humor and human interest.* When your listener smiles or laughs, it reduces tension. Humor is disarming and increases attention.
6. *One or two word pictures increase interest.* Don't just say, "Pat shared the gospel with me." You might briefly describe the setting so a person listening can visualize it.
7. Explain how Christ met or is meeting needs in your life, but *avoid implying that your struggles and problems ended at conversion.*
8. *Sound adult, not juvenile.* Reflect an adult point of view even if you were converted at an early age.
9. *Avoid dogmatic and mystical statements that skeptics can question,* such as "I prayed and God gave me a job" or "God said to me . . ."
10. *Simplify; reduce "clutter."* Mention a limited number of people and use only their first or last names. Combine information when you can.
    a. Poor: "Martha Smith, Nancy Van Buren, and her cousin Jane Matthews came by my office at Digital Binary Components Corporation."
    b. Good: "Martha and two other friends talked with me at work one day."

c. Good: "After living in five states and attending six universities, I finally graduated and got an engineering job."

DEVELOPING YOUR BEFORE, HOW, AND AFTER

Here are practical suggestions for developing the *before*, *how*, and *after* parts of your story.

1. Before:

   a. When non-Christians identify with your background, their interest grows. In "My Story," you can share one or more gaps or needs that characterized your pre-Christian life. Following are some common non-Christian life patterns or traits:

• no peace	• boredom	• can't shake bad habits
• fear of death	• loneliness	• no meaning to life
• guilt	• something missing	• emptiness
• no purpose	• depression	• dissatisfied with life

   b. Non-Christians may ignore or try to get rid of uncomfortable personal needs. Often their "solutions" don't work. As you develop your story, you might list positive as well as negative solutions that you tried, avoiding being graphic or detailed about sinful behavior. Consider touching on one or two items such as these:

• Marriage/family	• Sports/fitness	• Hobbies/entertainment
• Work	• Money	• Intimacy
• Drugs/alcohol	• Education	• Wrong friends

2. How:

   a. Describe circumstances that caused you to consider Christ. Perhaps identify events that led to your conversion. This may have taken place over a period of time.

   b. Briefly explain the specific steps you took to become a Christian. If there is a particular passage of Scripture that applies here, you may want to use it.

   c. Include the gospel clearly and briefly. The gospel includes:

1. All have sinned	3. Christ paid the penalty
2. Sin's penalty	4. Must receive Christ

3. After:
   a. Review the needs or life patterns you shared in your *before*. How has Christ helped or healed those sensitive or unpleasant needs? What has changed since becoming a follower of Christ (for example, knowing that your sins are forgiven, new meaning and purpose in life, assurance of salvation, or other ways your outlook has changed)?
   b. Conclude with a one-sentence statement about your confidence of having eternal life. The person you talk to will tend to comment on or remember the last thing you say.

TWO WAYS YOU MIGHT ORGANIZE YOUR STORY

On page 68, you will start considering which of three testimony formats you want to use for your salvation story. In addition to the three formats, here are options that many have found helpful. You might consider one of two ways to organize your story: either following the chronological sequence or using a quick overview/flashback as you begin your story.

1. Chronological
   In this approach, you tell your story in the chronological sequence in which it happened.

Before   After

Birth   Salvation   Now

   You might use this format:
   a. If you were converted later in life
   b. If you have enough interesting material to share prior to your conversion
   c. If your interesting *how* takes up a large portion of your story (the *before* then becomes relatively short).

2. Overview/Flashback
   In this approach, you give an interesting, rapid overview of your life right up to the present and then flash back to the spiritual dimension of your life. The flashback may go directly back to the *how* or to just preceding the *how*.

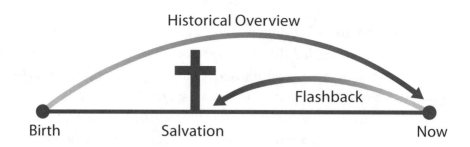

You might use this format:

a. If you came to Christ at an early age
b. If you had an uneventful early life but have had a more interesting adult life
c. If your *how* is very short

CHOOSING YOUR "MY STORY" FORMAT

SAMPLE FORMATS AND WORKSHEETS

Read through the three condensed sample salvation stories (pages 69–72). Then choose the format that best fits your own story and fill in the worksheet for that format (pages 72–76). As you write the first draft of your story, you may find it helpful to refer to the sample story and its worksheet that you filled out.

☐ **FORMAT 1: ADULT CONVERSION**

You trusted Christ as an adult. You have a distinct *before*, *how*, and *after*.

☐ **FORMAT 2: EARLY CONVERSION / ADULT DEEPER COMMITMENT**

You need to evaluate whether the early-conversion experience was genuine. If you conclude that it was not, then you might use Format 1 as your model. If it was genuine, your life may have been characterized by spiritual immaturity or a lifestyle similar to people without faith in Christ.

☐ **FORMAT 3: EARLY CONVERSION / CONSISTENT GROWTH**

You probably grew up with Christian parents and have a strong church background. You might have very little *before* to share. (Often the "overview/flashback" works well with this format.)

FORMAT 1:
ADULT CONVERSION*

BEFORE

A few years ago, I found myself lacking purpose in my life. Something was missing. Nothing seemed to fill the void. I had majored in electrical engineering in college and got a good job when I graduated. For three years, I put in extra hours and finally got a promotion, but I had no real satisfaction in that. I began working longer and longer hours, giving myself to my profession. This began to have a negative effect on me. I kept telling my wife that I was only doing it for her and the kids, but I knew that was a rationalization. What started out as the "ideal" marriage was coming apart at the seams. I got to the point that I did not want to go home at night. "Happy hour" was more fun than arguments.

HOW

In my next job, I was asked to attend an engineering seminar with David and Jack from work. David seemed to have a certain something that was missing in my life. On the way home from the seminar, David told me about how Christ had changed his life and had given him a whole new reason for living. Many of the things he said seemed to be similar to my situation. He talked about having been successful in business, but somehow he fell short of what he wanted out of life. Then he said that the answer to his frustration was to have personally committed his life to Jesus Christ. In a prayer, he'd admitted to God that he had done many things that he knew were very wrong. He had turned control of his life over to God. David told me that the Bible said that Christ had died on the cross so we could be forgiven for everything we had ever done wrong. I had heard this before, but now it seemed to make a lot more sense. A couple of days after the seminar, I took a walk down by the lake near our home. I prayed and confessed to God some of the things I had done that I knew had hurt and displeased Him. I asked Christ to come into my life and take over because I wasn't doing a very good job with it by myself.

---

*This is a condensed sample.

| AFTER | Well, there was no flash of light or strong emotion, but I do know that I felt as if a large weight was lifted from my shoulders. Not everything is perfect now, but I do feel as if I have a whole new purpose for living. God has given me more stability and purpose. It is now very important to me to know that I will be with God after this life. |

FORMAT 2:
EARLY CONVERSION / DEEPER ADULT COMMITMENT*

BEFORE FULL COMMITMENT	Not too long ago, you could have characterized my life as lacking any real inner peace. Everything around me seemed to be in utter turmoil. Nothing I did would ease the tension in my life. It didn't seem as if anything could fill the longing that was growing in my heart. I thought I could fill that emptiness by getting involved in activities. I joined the health spa, took golf lessons, and was involved in transporting our children to their various sports and lessons. I considered going back to work part-time. Then my husband received a promotion and we were transferred to another city. If I had felt tension before, the move just added to its intensity. It seemed that the only relief I found was from taking tranquilizers, but that was only temporary and it scared me to realize that I was beginning to depend on them.
HOW	We had gotten out of the habit of attending church over the years, but the Johnsons invited us to go to church with them, so we started going. After we had attended for a couple of months, we decided to participate in a Bible study group. There we met people who were fun but took their Christianity seriously. They began to encourage us to really commit our lives to Christ.
	We reviewed some things I had heard while growing up: that we were all breaking God's laws and deserved to be separated from Him but that God had provided the way to restore that relationship with Him and that provision was the death of His only Son, Jesus Christ. What I needed

*This is a condensed sample.

to do about it was to acknowledge my disobedience to God and turn from it and ask Christ to take over my life as my Savior and Lord. So I asked Christ to apply His death to me and to take over.

AFTER   It wasn't until we got involved in that Wednesday night Bible study that I really understood what it meant to be committed to Jesus Christ. I was learning that I couldn't experience inner peace while neglecting God. As a result of the Bible study, I made a whole new commitment to Christ. The inner peace that I was striving for so desperately was finally there. But the greatest thing of all is that I know for certain that I have a personal relationship with God through Christ and have eternal life.

FORMAT 3:
EARLY CONVERSION / CONSISTENT GROWTH*

BEFORE   As a single person, I see other singles feverishly trying to put together a happy, fulfilling life. They are into travel; some try the bar scene, dating, high-tech toys, sports, and even substance abuse. I also see married men and women (where I work) trying to put their lives together without really knowing how. I'm involved in many of the same social activities as other singles. I enjoy working out and running. I save up my money to take short overseas trips when I find a good price. But I have a contentment and stability that elude many people. This new stability began in my life during high school.

HOW   As I was growing up, my parents were very active in church. Because they were active, they figured that I should be also, so every Sunday, there we were. It was real for them, but for me it was just socializing with friends. Then one summer I attended a church camp. This changed my whole view of "religion." I discovered at this camp that Christianity was more than just a religion; it was a personal relationship with God through His Son, Jesus Christ.

*This is a condensed sample.

Some of the discussion groups centered around who Jesus Christ was and what He did. One day after sports, my camp counselor asked me if I had ever personally committed my life to Christ, or was I still thinking about it? I said that I was still thinking about it. We reviewed some key Bible verses about steps I could take to establish a meaningful relationship with God through Christ. From the Bible, I saw that I needed forgiveness and that God was offering the gift of eternal life. I put my trust in Jesus Christ's death on the cross for me. I said a prayer right there and asked Jesus Christ to apply His death on the cross to me personally.

AFTER As I grew physically and mentally, I also grew spiritually. I find that when I try to do things my way and leave God out of the picture, I have the same struggles as everyone else. But when I let Him be in control, I experience a stability that can come only from Him. The contentment I am experiencing through my relationship with God has impacted my job performance in positive ways and has helped me be less self-centered. But the greatest benefit is knowing that I have eternal life through Christ.

WORKSHEET — FORMAT 1: ADULT CONVERSION

Following is a list of questions for an Adult Conversion salvation story. Please jot down some of your thoughts under each question. This provides you a rough outline from which you can write sentences and paragraphs about your own experiences. This can help you put together your first draft of "My Story" to discuss in session 8.

BEFORE:

1. Before you met Christ, what were some of your needs, what was lacking, or what was missing in your life?

_____

_____

_____

2. What solutions for your life did you try that didn't work?

_____

_____

_____

HOW:

1. What were the circumstances that caused you to consider Christ?

_____

_____

_____

2. Tell how you trusted Christ, and briefly include the gospel.

_____

_____

_____

AFTER:

1. Give an example of how Christ met your needs or how He is now contributing to your life.

_____

_____

_____

2. End with a sentence to the effect that you know that you have eternal life through Christ.

_____

_____

_____

WORKSHEET — FORMAT 2:
EARLY CONVERSION / DEEPER ADULT COMMITMENT

Following is a list of questions for a story of Early Conversion / Deeper Adult Commitment. Please jot down some of your thoughts under each question. This provides you a rough outline from which you can write sentences and paragraphs about your own experiences. This can help you put together your first draft of "My Story" to discuss in session 8.

BEFORE:

1. Before your new commitment to Christ, what were some of your needs, what was lacking, or what was missing in your life?

_____

_____

_____

2. What solutions for your life did you try that didn't work?

_____

_____

_____

HOW:

1. What circumstances led you to make the deeper commitment to Christ?

_____

_____

2. Refer to your conversion experience, when you put your faith in Christ, and briefly include the gospel.

_____

_____

_____

AFTER:

1. Give an example of how Christ is meeting your needs or contributing to your life now.

_____

_____

_____

2. End with a sentence to the effect that you know that you have eternal life through Christ.

_____

_____

_____

WORKSHEET — FORMAT 3:
EARLY CONVERSION / CONSISTENT GROWTH

Following is a list of questions for an Early Conversion / Consistent Growth salvation story. Please jot down some of your thoughts under each question. This provides you a rough outline from which you can write sentences and paragraphs about your own experiences. This can help you put together your first draft of "My Story" to discuss in session 8.

BEFORE:

1. What are some needs or things missing that you have observed in other people?

_____

_____

_____

2. What solutions do you see that aren't working for people?

_____

_____

_____

HOW:

1. Explain how your relationship with God through Christ has made many of these things less of a problem for you.

_____

_____

2. Refer to your conversion experience. Briefly including the gospel, state how you trusted Christ.

_____

_____

_____

AFTER:

1. Give an example of how Christ is meeting your needs or contributing to your life.

_____

_____

2. End with a sentence to the effect that you know that you have eternal life through Christ.

_____

_____

_____

THE SESSION 8 WORKSHOP

You will find session 8 to be a very valuable experience. The workshop can be done in different ways, depending on the size of your church, the number of people in your group and other factors. The men and women responsible for your church's discipleship training will plan your workshop after considering options described at _www.2-7series.org_. Please pray for your leaders, for yourself, and for the others in your group—and that God will use session 8 in significant ways.

In whatever way session 8 is organized:

1. Plan to come to the workshop ready to read a written draft of your salvation story.
2. Come with a willingness to make adjustments in your story; others may suggest ways you might improve it. Everyone in your group will be rewriting parts of their story—sharpening it so that when told verbally, it can effectively impact the mind and heart of a non-Christian who hears it.

ASSIGNMENT FOR SESSION 8

1. Scripture Memory: Study and complete "Scripture Memory Guide—Week 8" (pages 79–80). Memorize the verse(s) on "Witnessing": Matthew 4:19 and Romans 1:16 (recommended but optional).
2. Quiet Time: Continue reading, marking, responding back to God in prayer, recording on *My Reading Highlights*, and using a prayer sheet.
3. My Story: Come with a written draft of your salvation story. Two things can be a great help to you:
   a. Write from the notes you made on one of the format worksheets (pages 72–76).
   b. Refer to the sample format that fits your story (page 69, 70, or 71).
4. Other: Work on getting everything completed that you can on *My Completion Record*.

SESSION 8

OUTLINE OF THIS SESSION

1. Open the session in prayer.
2. Read "Assignment for Session 9" (page 80).
3. Break into verse review groups and quote the verse(s) on "Witnessing": Matthew 4:19 and Romans 1:16 (recommended but optional).
4. Participate in the workshop for sharpening "My Story."
5. Close in prayer.

SCRIPTURE MEMORY GUIDE—WEEK 8

About the Verses

TOPIC 6: WITNESSING

God has given Christians the privilege and responsibility of reaching those who are without Christ. We are on earth to be His witnesses.

Matthew 4:19—Jesus challenged two fishermen with an infinitely greater goal: fishing for people. Whatever our occupation, Jesus wants us to follow Him and be involved with Him in reaching others with the gospel.

Romans 1:16 (recommended but optional)—Like the apostle Paul, we can share the gospel without embarrassment. It explains God's power to save—the eternal answer to the needs of men and women. Jesus said, "Whoever acknowledges me before others, I will also acknowledge before my Father in heaven" (Matthew 10:32).

The phrase "First to the Jew, then to the Gentile" (Romans 1:16) means that the gospel is for all people and has universal meaning and application.

Your Weekly Plan

1. For each verse you plan to memorize this week, have a card with the topic, reference, verse, and reference on one side and only the topic and reference on the other side.

2. Start memorizing Matthew 4:19, quoting the topic and reference and then adding one phrase at a time until you can quote the whole verse. When you are memorizing two verses in one week, you want to memorize the first verse in two days, then the second verse in two days, leaving three days to review them both.

3. Each day quote aloud the verses you memorized in book 1 along with your new book 2 verses.

4. Plan to carry your verse cards with you so you can use spare moments

during the day to memorize, review, or meditate on your verses.

5. Before coming to class, write out your new verse(s) from memory or quote your verse(s) to someone just to check accuracy.

ASSIGNMENT FOR SESSION 9

1. Scripture Memory: Continue to sharpen the verses you have learned. Review aloud whenever possible.

2. Quiet Time: Continue reading, marking, responding back to God in prayer, recording on *My Reading Highlights*, and using a prayer sheet.

3. My Story:

   a. Practice telling your story aloud using just your outline on an index card.

   b. Read the material on the lead-in and close to your salvation story (pages 81–82).

4. Other:

   a. Work on getting everything you can completed and ready to be signed on *My Completion Record*.

   b. Carefully read and mark *My Heart — Christ's Home* (pages 83–90) and complete "Discuss *My Heart — Christ's Home*" (pages 91–92).

SESSION 9

Please keep in mind that the lead-in and close you choose to use may vary with each person and situation.

LEAD-IN TO "MY STORY"

You have worked hard sharpening your salvation story. Questions might come to mind: "When do I share it?" "How do I direct the conversation so it will lead into telling 'My Story'?" Here are some suggestions (you are being wise and sensitive, not manipulative):

1. Include some small talk before discussing spiritual matters. Discuss family, job, hobbies, interests, and so on.
2. Be alert for needs expressed. Their felt need might become the basis for further discussion. Often being a good listener leads to your being able to share your story.
3. Discuss past concerns and needs that you had in your life, such as "We used to struggle in our marriage relationship" or "I used to allow the pressures at work to get to me, and then I discovered something that made a tremendous difference in my life."
4. Discuss contemporary situations happening in the news or in your area: "Recently I watched a video clip that showed the extent of substance abuse in small towns in America. It seems that people are trying to find

something that satisfies. People on the video explained how they slipped into that lifestyle." Avoid topics that lead to taking sides and arguing.

5. Build genuine friendships with them. It may take ten minutes, ten days, or ten months, but the investment of time can build a friendship.

6. Don't condemn them for behaving like non-Christians; they *are* non-Christians. You can be a friend without engaging in their marginal activities. As they continue to observe your life, they will see more and more how they can have a better life in Christ.

7. Avoid dogmatic "religious" statements, such as "God told me to _____" or "Jesus is the answer to all your problems." They don't yet know who He is, much less what He can do in their lives.

8. Avoid arguments on moral issues. You can expect non-Christians' views to conflict with clear biblical teaching. After their commitment to Christ, a biblical foundation can be established.

WAYS TO CLOSE "MY STORY"

When you have shared your salvation story, you may want to conclude with a statement that causes the person to reflect on what you just shared. What you will say depends on how the person has been responding to your testimony. If his or her response seems negative or neutral, you could say something like one of the following:

1. "Well, that's my story. Christ has really changed my life. Where are you in your thinking about God?"

2. "Have you wondered much about how a person can have eternal life?"

3. "If you are interested, maybe we could discuss this a little more sometime." If his or her response seems positive, you could ask one of these questions:
   a. "Bill, has anything like this ever happened to you?"
   b. "Mary, do you know for certain whether you have eternal life?"
   c. "What have you heard before about Christ's death on the cross?"
   d. "May I share an illustration with you that explains how a person can know for certain that they have eternal life?" (Perhaps use The Bridge Illustration if he or she says yes.)

Usually when you share "My Story," it is "planting and watering" (1 Corinthians 3:6-7), not "reaping" (John 4:36-38). "My Story" tends to be a door opener, not a convincing tool. A personal salvation story becomes the "bait," and the gospel is the "hook."

MY HEART — CHRIST'S HOME

Robert Boyd Munger

In his letter to the Ephesians, Paul writes these words: "That [God] may grant you to be strengthened with might through his Spirit in the inner man, and that Christ may dwell in your hearts through faith (Eph 3:16-17). Or, as another has translated, "That Christ may settle down and be at home in your hearts by faith" (Weymouth).

Without question, one of the most remarkable Christian doctrines is that Jesus Christ Himself through the Holy Spirit will actually enter a heart, settle down, and be at home there. Christ will live in any human heart that welcomes him.

He said to his disciples, "If a man loves me, he will keep my word, and my Father will love him, and we will come to him and make our home with him" (Jn 14:23). But he was also telling them that he was soon to leave them (Jn 13:33). It was difficult for them to understand what he was saying. How was it possible for him both to leave them and make his home with them at the same time?

It is interesting that Jesus uses a similar concept here *(home)* that he uses earlier in John 14: "I go to prepare a *place* for you . . . that where I am, you may be also" (vv. 2-3). He was promising that just as he was going to heaven to prepare a place for them and would one day welcome them there, so it would be possible for them to prepare a place for him in their hearts now. He would come and make his home with them right here.

This was beyond their comprehension. How could this be?

Then came Pentecost. The Spirit of the living Christ was given to the church and they experienced what he had foretold. Now they understood. God did not dwell in Herod's Temple in Jerusalem—nor in any temple made with hands! Now, through the miracle of the outpoured Spirit, God would dwell in human hearts. The body of the believer had become the temple of the living God and the human heart the home of Jesus Christ. Thirty minutes after Pentecost the disciples knew more about Jesus than they had known in the three years previously. It is difficult for me to think of a higher privilege than to make for Christ a home in my heart, to welcome, to serve, to please and to know him there.

I will never forget the evening I invited him into my heart. What an entrance he made! It was not a spectacular, emotional thing, but very real, occurring at the very center of my soul. He came into the darkness of my heart and turned on the light. He built a fire in the cold hearth and banished the chill. He started music where there had been stillness and harmony where there had been discord. He filled the emptiness with his own loving fellowship. I have never regretted opening the door to Christ and I never will.

This, of course, is the first step in making the heart Christ's home. He has said, "Behold, I stand at the door and knock; if anyone hears my voice and opens the door, I will come in to him and eat with him, and he with me" (Rev 3:20). If you want to know the reality of God and the personal presence of Jesus Christ at the innermost part of your being, simply open wide the door and ask him to come in and be your Savior and Lord.

After Christ entered my heart, in the joy of that new-found relationship, I said to him, "Lord, I want this heart of mine to be yours. I want you to settle down here and be fully at home. I want you to use it as your own. Let me show you around and point out some of the features of the home so that you may be more comfortable. I want you to enjoy our time together." He was glad to come and seemed delighted to be given a place in my ordinary little heart.

The Study

The first room we looked at together was the study—the library. Let us call it the study of the mind. Now in my home this room of the mind is a small room with thick walls. But it is an important room. In a sense, it is the control room of the house. He entered with me and looked around at the books in the bookcase, the magazines on the table, the pictures on the walls. As I followed his gaze, I became uncomfortable. Strangely enough, I had not felt bad about this room before, but now that he was there with me looking at these things, I was embarrassed. There were some books on the shelves his eyes were too pure to look at. On the table were a few magazines a Christian has no business reading. As for the pictures on the walls—the imaginations and thoughts of my mind—some of these were shameful.

Red-faced, I turned to him and said, "Master, I know this room really needs to be cleaned up and made over. Will you help me shape it up and change it to the way it ought to be?"

"Certainly," he replied, "I'm glad to help you! I've come to handle things like this! First of all, take all the materials you are reading and viewing which are not true, good, pure and helpful, and throw them out! Now put on the empty shelves the books of the Bible. Fill the library with the Scriptures and meditate on them day and night. As for the pictures on the walls, you will have difficulty controlling these images, but I have something that will help." He gave me a full-sized portrait of himself. "Hang this centrally," he said, "on the wall of the mind." I did, and I have discovered through the years that when my thoughts are centered on Christ, the awareness of his presence, purity and power causes wrong and impure thoughts to back away. So he has helped me to bring my thoughts under his control, but the struggle remains.

If you have difficulty with this little room of the mind, let me encourage you to bring Christ there. Pack it full with the Word of God, study it, meditate on it and keep clearly before you the presence of the Lord Jesus.

The Dining Room

From the study we went into the dining room, the room of appetites and desires. Now this was a large room, a most important place to me. I spent a lot of time and hard work trying to satisfy all my wants.

I told him, "This is a favorite room. I'm sure you will be pleased with what we serve here."

He seated himself at the table and inquired, "What is on the menu for dinner tonight?"

"Well," I said, "my favorite dishes: money, academic degrees, stocks, with newspaper articles of fame and fortune as "side dishes." These were the things I liked, thoroughly secular fare. There was nothing so very bad in any of them, but it was not really the kind of food which would feed the soul and satisfy true spiritual hunger.

When the plates were placed before my new friend, he said nothing. However, I observed that he did not eat. I asked, somewhat disturbed, "Savior, don't you like this food? What is the trouble?"

He answered, "I have food to eat you do not know of. My food is to do the will of him that sent me." He looked at me again and said, "If you want food that really satisfies you, do the will of your heavenly Father. Put his pleasure before your own. Stop striving for your own desires, your own ambitions, your own satisfactions. Seek to please him. That food will really satisfy you. Try a bit of it!"

And there about the table he gave me a taste of doing God's will. What flavor! There is no food like it in all the world. It alone satisfies. At the end everything else leaves you hungry.

What's the menu in the dining room of our desires? What kind of food are we serving our divine companion and serving ourselves? "All that is in the world, the lust of the flesh and the lust of the eyes and the pride of life" (1 Jn 2:16), our self-centered wants? Or are we finding God's will to be our soul-satisfying meat and drink?

The Living Room

We moved next into the living room. This was a quiet, comfortable room with a warm atmosphere. I liked it. It had a fireplace, sofa, overstuffed chairs, a bookcase and an intimate atmosphere.

He also seemed pleased with it. He said, "Indeed, this is a delightful room. Let's come here often. It's secluded and quiet, and we can have good talks and fellowship together."

Well, naturally, as a young

Christian I was thrilled. I couldn't think of anything I would rather do than have a few minutes alone with Christ in close companionship.

He promised, "I will be here every morning early. Meet me here and we will start the day together."

So, morning after morning, I would go downstairs to the living room. He would take a book of the Bible from the bookcase, open it, and we would read it together. He would unfold to me the wonder of God's saving truth recorded on its pages and make my heart sing as he shared all he had done for me and would be to me. Those times together were wonderful. Through the Bible and his Holy Spirit he would talk to me. In prayer I would respond. So our friendship deepened in these quiet times of personal conversation.

However, under the pressure of many responsibilities, little by little, this time began to be shortened. Why, I'm not sure. Somehow I assumed I was just too busy to give special, regular time to be with Christ. This was not a deliberate decision, you understand; it just seemed to happen that way. Eventually not only was the period shortened, but I began to miss days now and then, such as during midterms or finals. Matters of urgency demanding my attention were continually crowding out the quiet times of conversation with Jesus. Often I would miss it two days in a row or more.

One morning, I recall rushing down the steps in a hurry to be on my way to an important appointment.

As I passed the living room, the door was open. Glancing in I saw a fire in the fireplace and Jesus sitting there. Suddenly, in dismay, it came to me, "He is my guest. I invited him into my heart! He has come as my Savior and Friend to live with me. Yet here I am neglecting him."

I stopped, turned and hesitantly went in. With downcast glance I said, "Master, I'm sorry! Have you been here every morning?"

"Yes," he said, "I told you I would be here to meet with you." I was even more ashamed! He had been faithful in spite of my faithlessness. I asked him to forgive me and he did, as he always does when we acknowledge our failures and want to do the right thing.

He said, "The trouble is that you have been thinking of the quiet time, of Bible study and prayer, as a means for your own spiritual growth. This is true, but you have forgotten that this time means something to me also. Remember, I love you. At a great cost I have redeemed you. I value your fellowship. Just to have you look up into my face warms my heart. Don't neglect this hour if only for my sake. Whether or not you want to be with me, remember I want to be with you. I really love you!"

You know, the truth that Christ wants my fellowship, that he loves me, wants me to be with him and waits for me, has done more to transform my quiet time with God than any other single fact. Don't let Christ wait alone in the living room of your heart, but every day find a time and place when, with the Word of God and in prayer, you may be together with him.

The Workroom

Before long he asked, "Do you have a workroom in your house?"

Out in the garage of the home of my heart I had a workbench and some equipment, but I was not doing much with it. Once in a while I would play around at making a few little gadgets, but I wasn't producing anything substantial.

I took him out there.

He looked over the workbench and the few talents and skills I had. He said, "This is fairly well furnished. What are you producing with your life for the kingdom of God?" He looked at one or two of the little toys that I had thrown together on the bench and he held one up to me. "Is this the sort of thing you are doing for others in your Christian life?

I felt terrible! "Lord, that's the best I can do. I know it isn't much. I'm ashamed to say that with my awkwardness and limited ability, I don't think I'll ever do much more."

"Would you like to do better?" he asked.

"You know I would!" I replied.

"Well, first remember what I taught you: 'apart from me you can do nothing' (Jn 15:5).

"Come, relax in me and let my Spirit work through you. I know you are unskilled, clumsy and awkward, but the Spirit is the Master worker. If he controls your heart and your hands, he will work through you. Now turn around." Then putting his great strong arms around me and his hands under mine he picked up the tools and began to work through me. "Relax. You are still too tense. Let go—let me do the work!"

It amazes me what his skilled hands can do through mine if I only trust him and let him have his way. I am very far from satisfied with the product that is being turned out. I still get in his way at times. There's much more that I need to learn. But I do know that whatever has been produced for God has been through him and through the power of his Spirit in me.

Don't be discouraged because you cannot do much for God. It's not our ability but our availability that's important. Give what you are to Christ. Be sensitive and responsive to what he wants to do. Trust him. He will surprise you with what he can do through you!

The Rec Room

I remember the time he inquired about the rec room, where I went for fun and fellowship. I was hoping he would not ask me about that. There were certain associations and activities I wanted to keep for myself. I did not think Jesus would enjoy or approve of them. I evaded the question.

However, one evening when I was on my way out with some of my buddies for a night on the town, he was at the door and stopped me with a glance. "Are you going out?"

I answered, "Yes."

"Good," he said, "I would like to go with you."

"Oh," I replied rather awkwardly. "I don't think, Lord, that you would really enjoy where we are going. Let's go out together tomorrow night. Tomorrow night we can go do a Bible class or a social at the church, but tonight I have another engagement."

"As you wish," was his comment. "Only I thought when I came into your home we were going to do everything together—be close companions! Just know that I am willing to go with you!"

"Well," I said, "we'll go someplace together tomorrow night!

That evening I spent some miserable hours. I felt rotten! What kind of a friend was I to Jesus? Deliberately leaving him out of part of my life, doing things and going places that I knew very well he would not enjoy? When I returned that evening, there was a light in his room and I went up to talk it over with him. I acknowledged, "Lord, I have learned my lesson. I know now I can't have a good time if you are not along. From now on we will do everything together!"

Then we went down together into the rec room of the house. He transformed it. He brought new friendships, new excitement, new joys. Laughter and music have been ringing in the house ever since. With a twinkle in his eye, he smiled, "You thought that with me around you wouldn't have much fun, didn't you? Remember, I have come 'that my joy may be in you, and that your joy may be full'" (Jn 15:11).

The Bedroom

One day when we were in my bedroom he asked me about the picture next to my bed.

"That's a picture of my girlfriend," I told him. Though I knew my relationship with my girlfriend was a good one, I felt funny talking to him about it. She and I were struggling with some issues and I didn't want to discuss them with him. I tried to change the subject.

But Jesus must have known what I was thinking. "You are beginning to question my teaching on sex, aren't you? That intercourse is only for those who are joined in the covenant of marriage? You're feeling I may be asking something unnatural if not impossible for you. You're afraid my will on this will limit the full enjoyment of life and love. Isn't that true?"

"Yes," I confessed.

"Then listen carefully to what I am saying," he continued. "I forbid adultery and premarital sex not because sex is bad but because it is good. Beyond the physical ecstasy it is a means of bonding two lives in deepening love. It has the creative power to bring human life into being. Sex is powerful. Used properly sex has tremendous potential for good. Used improperly, it destroys the good. For this reason God intends it to be expressed only within the commitment of a loving life partnership. There is far more to love than just sex.

"Let me help you in your relationship with the opposite sex. If you should fail and feel shame and guilt, know I still love you and will remain with you. Talk to me about it! Acknowledge the wrong! Takes steps to avoid it happening again! Rely on my strength to keep you from falling and to lead you into a relationship of love in marriage where two truly become one in me.

The Hall Closet

There's one more matter of crucial consequence I would like to share with you. One day I found him waiting for me at the front door. An arresting look was in his eye. As I entered, he said to me, "There's a peculiar odor in the house. Something must be dead around here. It's upstairs. I think it is in the hall closet."

As soon as he said this I knew what he was talking about. Indeed there was a small closet up there on the hall landing, just a few feet square. In that closet behind lock and key I had one or two little personal things I

did not want anybody to know about. Certainly I did not want Christ to see them. They were dead and rotting things leftover from the old life—not wicked, but not right and good to have in a Christian life. Yet I loved them. I wanted them so much for myself I was really afraid to admit they were there. Reluctantly I went up the stairs with him and as we mounted, the odor became stronger and stronger. He pointed at the door and said, "It's in there! Some dead thing!"

It made me angry! That's the only way I can put it. I had given him access to the study, the dining room, the living room, the workroom, the rec room, the bedroom and now he was asking me about a little two-by-four closet. I said to myself, "This is too much! I am not going to give him the key."

"Well," he responded, reading my thoughts, "if you think I'm going to stay up here on the second floor with this smell, you are mistaken. I will take my bed out on the back porch or somewhere else. I'm certainly not going to stay around that." And I saw him start down the stairs.

When you have come to know and love Jesus Christ, one of the worst things that can happen is to sense him withdrawing his face and fellowship. I had to give in. "I'll give you the key," I said sadly, "but you'll have to open the closet and clean it out. I haven't the strength to do it."

"I know," he said. "I know you

haven't. Just give me the key. Just authorize me to handle that closet and I will." So, with trembling fingers, I passed the key over to him. He took it from my hand, walked over to the door, opened it, entered it, took out the putrefying stuff that was rotting there and threw it all away. Then he cleansed the closet, painted it and fixed it up all in a moment's time. Immediately a fresh, fragrant breeze swept through the house. The whole atmosphere changed. What release and victory to have that dead thing out of my life! No matter what sin or what pain there might be in my past, Jesus is ready to forgive, to heal and to make whole.

Transferring the Title

Then a thought came to me. I said to myself, "I have been trying to keep this heart of mine clean and available for Christ but it is hard work. I start on one room and no sooner have I cleaned it than I discover another room is dirty. I begin on the second room and the first one is already dusty again. I'm getting tired trying to maintain a clean heart and an obedient life. I just am not up to it!"

Suddenly I asked, "Lord, is there a possibility you would be willing to manage the whole house and operate it for me just as you did that closet? Could I give you the responsibility of keeping my heart what it ought to be and myself doing what I ought to be doing?"

I could see his face light up as he replied, "I'd love to! This is exactly what I came to do. You can't live out the Christian life in your own strength. That is impossible. Let me do it for you and through you. That's the only way it will really work! But," he added slowly, "I am not the owner of this house. Remember, I'm here as your guest. I have no authority to take charge since the property is not mine."

In a flash it all became clear. Excitedly I exclaimed, "Lord, you have been my guest, and I have been trying to play the host. From now on you are going to be the owner and master of the house. I'm going to be the servant!"

Running as fast as I could to the strongbox, I took out the title deed to the house describing its assets and liabilities, its condition, location and situation. Then rushing back to him, I eagerly signed it over giving title to him alone for time and eternity. Dropping to my knees, I presented it to him: "Here it is, all that I am and have forever. Now you run the house. Just let me stay with you as houseboy and friend."

He took my life that day and I can give you my word, there is no better way to live the Christian life. He knows how to keep it and use it. A deep peace settled down on my soul that has remained. I am his and he is mine forever!

May Christ settle down and be at home as Lord of your heart also.[4]

DISCUSS *MY HEART — CHRIST'S HOME*

Certainly, acknowledging Jesus Christ as Lord is a major step of commitment and surrender that every Christian will face at some point. Two verses that imply this are:

> Choose for yourselves this day whom you will serve. (Joshua 24:15)

> Dear brothers and sisters, I plead with you to give your bodies to God because of all he has done for you. Let them be a living and holy sacrifice—the kind he will find acceptable. This is truly the way to worship him. (Romans 12:1, NLT)

It is also true that Christ, as we allow Him, will increasingly take over our lives and gradually come to completely control them. This is the theme of *My Heart — Christ's Home*. The following verses emphasize that concept:

> I don't mean to say I am perfect. I haven't learned all I should even yet, but I keep working toward that day when I will finally be all that Christ saved me for and wants me to be. (Philippians 3:12, TLB)

> So all of us . . . can see and reflect the glory of the Lord. And the Lord—who is the Spirit—makes us more and more like him as we are changed into his glorious image. (2 Corinthians 3:18, NLT)

> Let us press on to know the LORD. His going forth is as certain as the dawn; and He will come to us like the rain, like the spring rain watering the earth. (Hosea 6:3, NASB)

Under the following eight headings, please jot down words and phrases that summarize the content of each of the eight topics in *My Heart — Christ's Home*.

THE STUDY _____

_____

THE DINING ROOM _____

_____

THE LIVING ROOM _____

_____

THE WORKROOM _____

_____

THE REC ROOM _____

_____

THE BEDROOM _____

_____

THE HALL CLOSET _____

_____

TRANSFERRING THE TITLE _____

_____

ASSIGNMENT FOR SESSION 10

1. Scripture Memory: Set aside a little extra review time to polish up all the verses you know.
2. Quiet Time: Continue reading, marking, responding, recording, and praying for people on your evangelism prayer lists.
3. My Story: If you haven't yet told your "My Story" to the group, come prepared to give it from an outline on an index card.
4. Other:
   a. Read and mark "Suggestions for Your Extended Time with God" (pages 93–105). Please leave "Highlights and Applications" blank (page 102).
   b. Decide what things you can have signed on *My Completion Record*.

SESSION 10

OUTLINE OF THIS SESSION

1. Open the session in prayer.
2. Break into verse review groups and quote all the verses you have learned in book 2.
3. Share some quiet-time thoughts, primarily from *My Reading Highlights*.
4. Tell your "My Story" from an outline on an index card.
5. Briefly, what has resulted from using your prayer sheets?
6. Confirm the time and place for session 11, your Extended Time with God.
7. Discuss "Suggestions for Your Extended Time with God" (pages 93–105), which include:
   a. *How to Spend a Day in Prayer* (pages 94–101)
   b. "Ways to Stay Awake and Alert" (page 102)
   c. "Making a Worry List" (pages 102–103)
   d. "Checklist for Your Extended Time with God" (pages 103–104)
   e. "Sample of Note-Taking During an Extended Time with God" (pages 104–105)
8. Read "Assignment for Session 11" (page 105).
9. Close in prayer. Focus on people on your evangelism prayer list and any upcoming friendship activities.

SUGGESTIONS FOR YOUR EXTENDED TIME WITH GOD

During session 11, everyone in your group has the opportunity to spend a block of time alone with God. The group is together for a brief time at the beginning and at the end of your individual Extended Time with God.

Not even a half-day is scheduled for your time with God, but as you read and mark *How to Spend a Day in Prayer*, you will find options and ideas that you can apply to your Extended Time with God in session 11. Other practical suggestions are discussed in this session as well.

HOW TO SPEND A DAY IN PRAYER

Lorne C. Sanny

"Avail yourself of the greatest privilege this side of heaven. Jesus Christ died to make this communion and communication with the Father possible."

— BILLY GRAHAM

"Prayer is a powerful thing, for God has bound and tied Himself thereto."

— MARTIN LUTHER

"God's acquaintance is not made hurriedly. He does not bestow His gifts on the casual or hasty comer and goer. To be much alone with God is the secret of knowing Him and of influence with Him."

— E. M. BOUNDS

"I never thought a day could make such a difference," a friend said to me. "My relationship to everyone seems improved."

"Why don't I do it more often?"

Comments like these come from those who set aside a personal day of prayer.

With so many activities—important ones—clamoring for our time, real prayer is considered more a luxury than a necessity. How much more so spending a *day* in prayer!

The Bible gives us three time-guides for personal prayer. There is the command to "pray without ceasing"—the spirit of prayer—keeping so in tune with God that we can lift our hearts in request or praise anytime through the day.

There is also the practice of a quiet time or morning watch—seen in the life of David (Psalm 5:3), of Daniel (6:10), and of the Lord Jesus (Mark 1:35). This daily time specified for meditation in the Word of God and prayer is indispensable to the growing, healthy Christian.

Then there are examples in the Scripture of extended time given to prayer alone. Jesus spent whole nights praying. Nehemiah prayed "certain days" upon hearing of the plight of Jerusalem. Three times Moses spent forty days and forty nights alone with God.

Learning from God

I believe it was in these special times of prayer that God made known His ways and His plans to Moses (Psalm 103:7). He allowed Moses to look through a chink in the fence and gain special insights, while the rank-and-file Israelites saw only the *acts* of God as they unfolded day by day.

Once I remarked to Dawson Trotman, founder of The Navigators, "You impress me as one who feels he is a man of destiny, one destined to be used of God."

"I don't think that's the case," he replied, "but I know this. God *has* given me some promises that I know He will fulfill." During earlier years Dawson spent countless protracted times alone with God, and out of these times the Navigator work grew—not by methods or principles but by promises given to him from the Word.

In my own life one of the most refreshing and stabilizing factors, as well as the means for new direction or confirmation of the will of God, has been those extended times of prayer—in the neighborhood park in Seattle, on a hill behind the Navigator home in Southern California, or out in the Garden of the Gods here in Colorado Springs.

These special prayer times can become anchor points in your life, times when you "drive a stake" as a landmark and go on from there. Your daily quiet time is more effective as you pray into day-by-day reality some of the things the Lord speaks to your heart in protracted times of prayer. The quiet time, in turn, is the foundation for "praying without ceasing," going through the day in communion with God.

Perhaps you haven't spent a protracted time in prayer because you haven't recognized the need for it. Or maybe you aren't sure what you would do with a whole day on your hands *just to pray.*

Why a Day of Prayer?

Why take this time from a busy life? What is it for?

1. *For extended fellowship with God*—beyond your morning devotions. It means just plain being with and thinking about God.

God has called us into fellowship of His Son, Jesus Christ (1 Corinthians 1:9). Like many personal relationships, this fellowship is nurtured by spending time together. God takes special note of times when His people reverence Him and *think upon His Name* (Malachi 3:16).

2. *For a renewed perspective.* Like flying over the battlefield in a reconnaissance plane, a day of prayer gives opportunity to think of the world from God's point of view. Especially when going through some difficulty, we need this perspective to sharpen our vision of the unseen and to let the immediate, tangible things drop into proper place. Our spiritual defenses are strengthened while "we fix our eyes not on what is seen, but on what is unseen, since . . . what is unseen is eternal" (2 Corinthians 4:18).

3. *For catching up on intercession.* There are non-Christian friends and relatives to bring before the Lord, missionaries on various fields, our pastors, neighbors, and Christian associates, our government leaders—to name a few. Influencing people and changing events through prayer is well known among Christians but too little practiced. And as times become more

serious around us, we need to reconsider the value of personal prayer, both to accomplish and to deter.

4. *For prayerful consideration of our own lives before the Lord*—personal inventory and evaluation. You will especially want to take a day of prayer when facing important decisions, as well as on a periodic basis. On such a day you can evaluate where you are in relation to your goals and get direction from the Lord through His Word. Promises are there for you and me, just as they have been for Hudson Taylor or George Mueller or Dawson Trotman. And it is in our times alone with God that He gives inner assurance of His promises to us.

5. *For adequate preparation.* Nehemiah, after spending "certain days" seeking the Lord in prayer, was called in before the king. "Then the king said unto me, For what dost thou make request? So I prayed to the God of heaven. And I said unto the king, 'If it please the king . . .'"—and he outlined his plan (Nehemiah 2:4-5, KJV). Then Nehemiah says, "I set out during the night with a few others. I had not told anyone what my God had put in my heart to do for Jerusalem" (2:12). When did God put in Nehemiah's heart this plan? I believe it was when he fasted and prayed and waited on God. Then when the day came for action, he was ready.

I heard a boy ask a pilot if it took quick thinking to land his plane when something went wrong. The pilot answered that no, he knew at all times where he would put down *if* something went wrong. He had that thought out ahead of time.

So it should be in our Christian life. If God has given us plans and purposes in those times alone, we will be ready when opportunity comes to move right into it. We won't have to say, "I'm not prepared." The reason many Christians are dead to opportunities is not because they are not mentally alert, but they are simply unprepared in heart. Preparation is made when we get alone with God.

Pray on the Basis of God's Word

Daniel said, "In the first year of [Darius's] reign, I, Daniel, understood from the Scriptures, according to the word of the LORD given to Jeremiah the prophet, that the desolation of Jerusalem would last seventy years. So I turned to the Lord God and pleaded with him in prayer and petition, in fasting, and in sackcloth and ashes. I prayed to the LORD my God and confessed" (Daniel 9:2-4).

He understood by the Scriptures what was to come. And as a result of his exposure to the Word of God, he prayed. It has been said that God purposes, therefore He promises. And we can add, "Therefore I pray the promises, so that God's purposes might come to reality." God purposed to do something, and He promised it; therefore, Daniel prayed. This was Daniel's part in completing the circuit, like an electrical circuit, so that the power could flow through.

Your day alone with the Lord isn't a matter of sitting out on a rock like a statue of *The Thinker* and taking whatever thoughts come to your mind. That's not safe. It should be a day exposed to God's Word, and then His Word leads you into prayer. You will end the day worse than you started if all you do is engage in introspection, thinking of yourself and your own problems. It isn't your estimate of yourself that counts anyway. It's God's estimate. And He will reveal His estimate to you by the Holy Spirit through His Word, the open Bible. And then the Word leads into prayer.

How to Go About it

How do you go about it? Having set aside a day or portion of a day for prayer, pack a lunch and start out. Find a place where you can be alone, away from distractions. This may be a wooded area near home or your backyard. An outdoor spot is excellent if you can find it, but don't get sidetracked into nature studies and fritter away your time. If you find yourself watching the squirrels or the ants, direct your observation by reading Psalm 104 and meditating on the power of God in creation.

Take along a Bible, a notebook and pencil, a hymnbook, and perhaps a devotional book. I like to have with me the booklet *Power Through Prayer* by E. M. Bounds and read a chapter or

two as a challenge to the strategic value of prayer. Or I sometimes take Horatius Bonar's *Words to Winners of Souls*, or a missionary biography like *Behind the Ranges*, which records the prayer victories of J. O. Fraser in inland China

Even if you have all day, you will want to use it profitably. So lose no time in starting, and start purposefully.

Wait on the Lord

Divide the day into three parts: waiting on the Lord, prayer for others, and prayer for yourself.

As you *wait on the Lord*, don't hurry. You will miss the point if you look for some mystical or ecstatic experience. Just seek the Lord, waiting on him. Isaiah 40:31 promises that those who wait upon the Lord will renew their strength. Psalm 27:14 is one of dozens of verses that mention waiting on Him, as is Psalm 62:5 — "Yes, my soul, find rest in God; my hope comes from him."

Wait on Him first *to realize His presence*. Read through a passage like Psalm 139, grasping the truth of His presence with you as you read each verse. Ponder the impossibility of being anywhere in the universe where He is not. Often we are like Jacob when he said, "Surely the LORD is in this place; and I knew it not" (Genesis 28:16, KJV).

Wait on Him also *for cleansing*. The last two verses of Psalm 139 lead you into this. Ask God to search your heart as these verses suggest. When we search our own hearts it can lead to imaginations, morbid introspection, or anything the enemy may want to throw before us. But when the Holy Spirit searches He will bring to your attention that which should be confessed and cleansed. Psalms 51 and 32, David's songs of confession, will help you. Stand upon the firm ground of 1 John 1:9 and claim God's faithfulness to forgive whatever specific thing you confess.

If you realize you've sinned against a brother, make a note of it so you won't forget to set it right. Otherwise, the rest of the day will be hindered. God won't be speaking to you if there is something between you and someone else that you haven't planned to take care of at the earliest possible moment.

As you wait on God, ask for the power of concentration. Bring yourself back from daydreaming.

Next, wait on God *to worship Him*. Psalms 103, 111, and 145 are wonderful portions to follow as you praise the Lord for the greatness of His power. Most of the psalms are prayers. Or turn to Revelation, chapters 4 and 5, and use them in your praise to Him. There is no better way to pray scripturally than to pray Scripture.

If you brought a hymnbook you can sing to the Lord. Some wonderful hymns have been written that put into words what we could scarcely express ourselves. Maybe you don't sing very well—then be sure you're

out of earshot of someone else and "make a joyful noise unto the Lord." *He* will appreciate it.

This will lead you naturally into thanksgiving. Reflect upon the wonderful things God has done for you and thank Him for these—for your own salvation and spiritual blessings, for your family, friends, and opportunities. Go beyond that which you thank the Lord for daily, and take time to express appreciation to Him for countless things He's given.

Prayer for Others

Now is the time for the unhurried, more detailed prayer for others that you don't get to ordinarily. Remember people in addition to those for whom you usually pray. Trace your way around the world, praying for people by countries.

Here are three suggestions for what to pray:

First, ask specific things for them. Perhaps you remember or have jotted down various needs people have mentioned. Use requests from missionary prayer letters. Pray for spiritual strength, courage, physical stamina, mental alertness, and so on. Imagine yourself in the situations where these people are and pray accordingly.

Second, look up some of the prayers in Scripture. Pray what Paul prayed for other people in the first chapter of Philippians and Colossians, and in the first and third chapters of Ephesians. This will help you advance in your prayer from the stage of "Lord, bless so and so and help them to do such and such."

Third, ask for others what you are praying for yourself. Desire for them what the Lord has shown *you*.

If you pray a certain verse or promise of Scripture for a person, you may want to put the reference by his name on your prayer list. Use this verse as you pray for that person the next time. Then use it for thanksgiving as you see the Lord answer.

Prayer for Yourself

The third part of your day will be prayer for yourself. If you are facing an important decision you may want to put this before prayer for others.

Again, let your prayer be ordered by Scripture, and ask the Lord for understanding according to Psalm 119:18. Meditate upon verses of Scripture you have memorized or promises you have previously claimed from the Word. Reading a whole book of the Bible through, perhaps aloud, is a good idea. Consider how it might apply to your life.

In prayer for yourself, 1 Chronicles 4:10 is one good example to follow. Jabez prayed, "Oh, that you would bless me and enlarge my territory! Let your hand be with me, and keep me from harm so that I will be free from pain." That's prayer for your personal life, your growth, God's presence, and God's protection. Jabez prayed in the will of God, and God granted his request.

"Lord, what do *You* think of my life?" is the attitude of this portion of your day of prayer. Consider your main objectives in the light of what you know to be God's will for you. Jesus said, "My food . . . is to do the will of him who sent me and to finish his work" (John 4:34). Do you want to do God's will more than anything else? Is it really your highest desire?

Then consider your activities—what you *do*—in the context of your objectives. God may speak to you about rearranging your schedule, cutting out certain activities that are good but not best, or some things that are entanglements or impediments to progress. Strip them off. You may be convicted about how you spend your evenings or Saturdays, when you could use the time to your advantage and still get the recreation you need.

As you pray, record your thoughts on your activities and use of time, and plan for better scheduling. Perhaps the need for better preparation for your Sunday school class or a personal visit with an individual will come to your mind. Or the Lord may impress you to do something special for someone. Make a note of it.

During this part of your day, bring up any problems or decisions you are facing and seek the mind of God on them. It helps to list the factors involved in these decisions or problems. Pray over these factors and look into the Scriptures for guidance. You may be led to a promise or direction from the passages with which you have already filled your mind during the day.

After prayer, you may reach some definite conclusions upon which you can base firm convictions. It should be your aim in a day of prayer to come away with some conclusions and specific direction—some stakes driven. However, do not be discouraged if this is not the case. It may not be God's time for a conclusive answer to your problem. And you may discover that your real need was not to know the next step but to have a new revelation of God Himself.

In looking for promises to claim there's no need to thumb through looking for new or startling ones. Just start with the promises you already know. If you have been through the Topical Memory System, start by meditating on the verses in the "Rely on God's Resources" section. Chew over some old familiar promises the Lord has given you before, ones you remember as you think back. Pray about applying these verses to your life.

I have found some of the greatest blessings from a new realization of promises I already knew. And the familiar promises may lead you to others. The Bible is full of them.

You may want to mark or underline in your Bible the promises the Lord gives during these protracted times alone. Put the date and a word or two in the margin beside them.

Variety is important during your day of prayer. Read a while, pray awhile, then walk around. A friend of mine paces the floor of his room for his prayer time. Rather than get cramped in one position, take a walk and stretch; add some variety.

As outside things pop into your mind, simply incorporate those items into prayer. If it's some business item you must not forget, jot it down. Have you noticed how many things come to mind while you are sitting in church? It will be natural for things to occur to you during your prayer day that you should have done, so put them down, pray about them and plan how you can take care of them and when. Don't just push them aside or they will plague you the rest of the day.

At the end of the day summarize in your notebook some things God has spoken to you about. This will be profitable to refer to later.

Two Questions

The result of your day of prayer should be answers to the two questions Paul asked the Lord on the Damascus road (Acts 22:6-10). Paul's first question was, "Who are you, Lord?" The Lord replied, "I am Jesus." You will be seeking to know Him, to find out who He is. The second question Paul asked was, "What shall I do, Lord?" The Lord answered him specifically. This should be answered or reconfirmed for you in that part of the day when you unhurriedly seek His will for you.

Don't think you must end the day with some new discovery or extraordinary experience. Wait on God and expose yourself to His Word. Looking for a new experience or insight you can share with someone when you get back will get you off track. True, you may gain some new insight, but often this can just take your attention from the real business. The test of such a day is not how exhilarated we are when the day is over but how it works into life tomorrow. If we have really exposed ourselves to the Word and come into contact with God, it will affect our daily life.

Days of prayer don't just happen. Besides the attempts of our enemy Satan to keep us from praying, the world around us has plenty to offer to fill our time. So we have to *make* time. Plan ahead—the first of every other month, or once a quarter.

God bless you as you do this—and do it soon! You too will probably ask yourself, "Why not more often?"[5]

> I love the LORD, for he heard my voice;
> > he heard my cry for mercy.
> Because he turned his ear to me,
> > I will call on him as long as I live. . . .
> I will sacrifice a thank offering to you
> > and call on the name of the LORD. (Psalm 116:1-2,17)

How to Spend a Day in Prayer suggests a three-part Extended Time with God. You may choose to use all or part of the outline.

1. Wait on the Lord:
   a. To realize His presence
   b. To be cleansed
   c. To worship Him
2. Pray for others:
   a. Ask specific things for them.
   b. Use Paul's prayers for others.
   c. Ask for others what you are praying for yourself.
3. Pray for yourself:
   a. Guidance and wisdom
   b. Godliness
   c. Concerns and needs

HIGHLIGHTS AND APPLICATIONS

(YOUR NOTES AS YOU AND YOUR GROUP DISCUSS *HOW TO SPEND A DAY IN PRAYER*)

_____

_____

_____

_____

_____

_____

_____

_____

_____

_____

WAYS TO STAY AWAKE AND ALERT

1. Get adequate rest the two nights before your Extended Time with God.
2. Change positions (sit a while, walk around, and so on).
3. Have variety in what you do (read the Scriptures a while, pray, plan or organize, and so on).
4. Pray aloud, in a whisper or soft voice. Sometimes thinking aloud also helps.

MAKING A WORRY LIST

Problems and concerns frequently cross our minds. Preparing a worry list can reduce those recurring thoughts and move us toward solutions to those issues. You may want to try the following suggestions for preparing your own worry list:

1. Give some thought to current conflicts, problems, concerns, or frustrations. List everything that troubles you. Number each of the items. No matter how small an issue is, if it is a concern to you, list it. Ask God to reveal to you anything else that is a point of concern.
2. Every worry that you have in the world should be on that list. Nothing

else concerns you—it is all there! When you are satisfied that all your concerns are listed, move on to step 3.

3. Go through the list item by item. On each item, you will conclude either that you can do nothing about it because it is past or beyond your control or that you can do something toward resolving that issue. If there is nothing you can do about a given item, spend some time in prayer about it. If you feel that you can take action on a particular item, still pray about it and then make a "do list" of one or two things you plan to do specifically to help resolve it. After you have gone through many of these concerns, you will have several items on a "do list." During your Extended Time with God, you might come up with other things you want to put on your "do list."

4. It may be wise to dispose of your worry list if it contains people's names or personal issues that should be kept private. It is not uncommon for an individual to have about twenty items on a worry list when it is compiled on a monthly basis.

CHECKLIST FOR YOUR EXTENDED TIME WITH GOD

(Other resources and options are listed at www.2-7series.org.)
1. Essential
   a. A Bible (perhaps the one you read regularly)
   b. A notebook, paper, or laptop for taking notes
   c. Pens or pencils
   d. A way to keep track of time (for example, a cell phone with the ringer off or a watch)
2. Optional
   a. Prayer letters from missionaries or Christian workers
   b. A devotional book such as:
      (1) *Power Through Prayer*, by E. M. Bounds
      (2) *Words to Winners of Souls*, by Horatius Bonar
      (3) *Prayer: Conversing with God*, by Rosalind Rinker
      (4) *The Practice of the Presence of God*, by Brother Lawrence
      (5) *Pray: How to be Effective in Prayer*, by Warren and Ruth Myers
      (6) *Purpose in Prayer*, by E. M. Bounds
   c. A sack lunch and beverage
   d. Your current prayer list
   e. Memory cards, for putting in some extra review and meditation time or for praying about these verses

f. Your *My Reading Highlights* from recent weeks, in order to look for trends of how God is "speaking" to you

g. Comfortable clothing appropriate for the temperature and location

h. A calendar of the months ahead

i. A hymnbook

j. Notes from your last Extended Time with God

k. Your list of objectives or goals

l. Facts about a decision you are making

m. A copy of your weekly schedule

SAMPLE OF NOTE-TAKING DURING AN EXTENDED TIME WITH GOD

Time	Notes	Duration
1:15–1:45	John 14–16	30 min
	14:3 Heaven is still being prepared	
	14:13 Jesus' involvement in prayer	
	14:15,21 Obey! (15:7,10)	
	16:26 "Then you shall present your petitions over my signature."	
1:45–1:50	Confession time	5 min
1:50–2:00	Reviewing "How to Spend a Day in Prayer"	10 min
2:00–2:15	Psalm 145—Reading, Praise, Worship	15 min
	145:3,6 We have a great God!	
	145:4 He will work with my children	
	145:9 I'm thankful for God's mercy!	
	145:15 God meets needs—He has met mine!	
	145:17 I want to grow in holiness	
2:15–3:00	Making a "Worry List" (prayer and do list)	45 min
3:00–3:20	Prayer for other people	20 min

~~~~~~~~~~~~~~~~~~~~~~~~~~~~~~~~~~~

Do List:
1. Organize Prayer Sheets
2. Apologize to _____ about _____
3. Clean out car trunk

~~~~~~~~~~~~~~~~~~~~~~~~~~~~~~~~~~~

4:00–4:20	Conclusions	20 min
	1. Quiet time and memory review must be daily things I "never" miss!	
	2. Pray and work toward a _balanced_ life!	

ASSIGNMENT FOR SESSION 11

1. Scripture Memory: Spend some time quoting and thinking about the verses you have learned in books 1 and 2.

2. Quiet Time: Continue reading, marking, responding back to God in prayer, recording on *My Reading Highlights*, and using a prayer sheet.

3. Extended Time with God:

   a. Make your choices from the checklist (pages 103–104) and come rested, alert, and eager to spend time with God.

   b. Your group leader will explain how session 11 will be done based on his or her planning and the suggestions given at www.2-7series.org.

4. Other: Have remaining book 2 items signed off on *My Completion Record*.

SESSION 11

EXTENDED TIME WITH GOD

The discipleship leaders in your church and your group leader will plan this workshop in a way that they believe will be most beneficial to all who participate in it.

Enjoy your extended time with God!

THE CHALLENGE CONTINUES . . .

While going through *Deepening Your Roots in God's Family* (book 2), you have further developed your walk with Christ by:

- Studying suggestions and options for an Extended Time with God
- Experiencing Extended Time with God
- Learning how to prepare and present "My Story" (how Christ has worked in your life)
- Reading about and discussing the lordship of Christ in a Christian's life
- Memorizing valuable verses on "Live the New Life."
- Studying scriptural principles for walking with Christ

A PREVIEW OF BOOK 3

Now that you have completed book 2, consider continuing with the next excellent discipleship training segment, *Bearing Fruit in God's Family*.

- Book 1: Growing Strong in God's Family
- Book 2: Deepening Your Roots in God's Family
- Book 3: Bearing Fruit in God's Family

In book 3, you will continue to develop and strengthen your walk with Christ by:

- Memorizing key verses on "Proclaim Christ," verses you can use for explaining the gospel to someone

- Telling your "My Story" with or without outline notes in less than four minutes
- Learning how to use The Bridge Illustration to visually and verbally explain the gospel
- Discussing two training segments on ways to apply priorities to everyday living
- Studying scriptural principles related to Christian character

We hope you plan to continue in THE 2:7 SERIES training process. Can you commit yourself to working through book 3 and completing this excellent training? If you do, most likely you will enjoy benefits for a lifetime!

APPENDIX

- My Reading Highlights
- Prayer Sheets

MY READING HIGHLIGHTS

"Now, my children, listen to me. Those who follow my ways are happy. Listen to my teaching, and you will be wise. Do not ignore it. Those who listen to me are happy. They stand watching at my door every day. They are at my open door waiting to be with me." —Proverbs 8:32-34 (NCV)

Translation _____ Year _____

☐ **Sunday** Date _____ All I read today _____

Best thing I marked today: *Reference* _____

Thought: _____

_____

How it impressed me: _____

_____

_____

_____

☐ **Monday** Date _____ All I read today _____

Best thing I marked today: *Reference* _____

Thought: _____

_____

How it impressed me: _____

_____

_____

_____

_____

☐ **Tuesday** Date _____ All I read today _____

Best thing I marked today: *Reference* _____

Thought: _____

_____

How it impressed me: _____

_____

_____

_____

☐ **Wednesday** Date_____ All I read today _____

Best thing I marked today: *Reference* _____

Thought: _____

_____

How it impressed me: _____

_____

_____

_____

☐ **Thursday** Date _____ All I read today _____

Best thing I marked today: *Reference* _____

Thought: _____

_____

How it impressed me: _____

_____

_____

_____

_____

☐ **Friday** Date _____ All I read today _____

Best thing I marked today: *Reference* _____

Thought: _____

_____

How it impressed me: _____

_____

_____

_____

☐ **Saturday** Date _____ All I read today _____

Best thing I marked today: *Reference* _____

Thought: _____

_____

How it impressed me: _____

_____

_____

_____

MY READING HIGHLIGHTS

"Now, my children, listen to me. Those who follow my ways are happy. Listen to my teaching, and you will be wise. Do not ignore it. Those who listen to me are happy. They stand watching at my door every day. They are at my open door waiting to be with me." —Proverbs 8:32-34 (NCV)

Translation _____ Year _____

☐ **Sunday** Date _____ All I read today _____

Best thing I marked today: *Reference* _____

Thought: _____

_____

How it impressed me: _____

_____

_____

☐ **Monday** Date _____ All I read today _____

Best thing I marked today: *Reference* _____

Thought: _____

_____

How it impressed me: _____

_____

_____

_____

☐ **Tuesday** Date _____ All I read today _____

Best thing I marked today: *Reference* _____

Thought: _____

_____

How it impressed me: _____

_____

_____

☐ **Wednesday** Date_____ All I read today _____

Best thing I marked today: *Reference* _____

Thought: _____

_____

How it impressed me: _____

_____

_____

_____

☐ **Thursday** Date_____ All I read today _____

Best thing I marked today: *Reference* _____

Thought: _____

_____

How it impressed me: _____

_____

_____

_____

_____

☐ **Friday** Date_____ All I read today _____

Best thing I marked today: *Reference* _____

Thought: _____

_____

How it impressed me: _____

_____

_____

_____

☐ **Saturday** Date_____ All I read today _____

Best thing I marked today: *Reference* _____

Thought: _____

_____

How it impressed me: _____

_____

_____

_____

MY READING HIGHLIGHTS

"Now, my children, listen to me. Those who follow my ways are happy. Listen to my teaching, and you will be wise. Do not ignore it. Those who listen to me are happy. They stand watching at my door every day. They are at my open door waiting to be with me." —Proverbs 8:32-34 (NCV)

Translation _____ Year _____

☐ **Sunday** Date _____ All I read today _____

Best thing I marked today: *Reference* _____

Thought: _____

_____

How it impressed me: _____

_____

_____

☐ **Monday** Date _____ All I read today _____

Best thing I marked today: *Reference* _____

Thought: _____

_____

How it impressed me: _____

_____

_____

_____

☐ **Tuesday** Date _____ All I read today _____

Best thing I marked today: *Reference* _____

Thought: _____

_____

How it impressed me: _____

_____

_____

☐ **Wednesday** Date_____ All I read today _____

Best thing I marked today: *Reference* _____

Thought: _____

_____

How it impressed me: _____

_____

_____

_____

☐ **Thursday** Date _____ All I read today _____

Best thing I marked today: *Reference* _____

Thought: _____

_____

How it impressed me: _____

_____

_____

_____

☐ **Friday** Date _____ All I read today _____

Best thing I marked today: *Reference* _____

Thought: _____

_____

How it impressed me: _____

_____

_____

_____

☐ **Saturday** Date _____ All I read today _____

Best thing I marked today: *Reference* _____

Thought: _____

_____

How it impressed me: _____

_____

_____

_____

MY READING HIGHLIGHTS

"Now, my children, listen to me. Those who follow my ways are happy. Listen to my teaching, and you will be wise. Do not ignore it. Those who listen to me are happy. They stand watching at my door every day. They are at my open door waiting to be with me." —Proverbs 8:32-34 (NCV)

Translation _____ Year _____

☐ **Sunday** Date _____ All I read today _____

Best thing I marked today: *Reference* _____

Thought: _____

_____

How it impressed me: _____

_____

_____

_____

☐ **Monday** Date _____ All I read today _____

Best thing I marked today: *Reference* _____

Thought: _____

_____

How it impressed me: _____

_____

_____

_____

☐ **Tuesday** Date _____ All I read today _____

Best thing I marked today: *Reference* _____

Thought: _____

_____

How it impressed me: _____

_____

_____

_____

☐ **Wednesday** Date _____ All I read today _____

Best thing I marked today: *Reference* _____

Thought: _____

_____

How it impressed me: _____

_____

_____

_____

☐ **Thursday** Date _____ All I read today _____

Best thing I marked today: *Reference* _____

Thought: _____

_____

How it impressed me: _____

_____

_____

_____

☐ **Friday** Date _____ All I read today _____

Best thing I marked today: *Reference* _____

Thought: _____

_____

How it impressed me: _____

_____

_____

_____

☐ **Saturday** Date _____ All I read today _____

Best thing I marked today: *Reference* _____

Thought: _____

_____

How it impressed me: _____

_____

_____

_____

MY READING HIGHLIGHTS

"Now, my children, listen to me. Those who follow my ways are happy. Listen to my teaching, and you will be wise. Do not ignore it. Those who listen to me are happy. They stand watching at my door every day. They are at my open door waiting to be with me." —Proverbs 8:32-34 (NCV)

Translation _____ Year _____

☐ **Sunday** Date _____ All I read today _____

Best thing I marked today: *Reference* _____

Thought: _____

_____

How it impressed me: _____

_____

_____

_____

☐ **Monday** Date _____ All I read today _____

Best thing I marked today: *Reference* _____

Thought: _____

_____

How it impressed me: _____

_____

_____

_____

☐ **Tuesday** Date _____ All I read today _____

Best thing I marked today: *Reference* _____

Thought: _____

_____

How it impressed me: _____

_____

_____

_____

☐ **Wednesday** Date_____ All I read today _____

Best thing I marked today: *Reference* _____

Thought: _____

How it impressed me: _____

☐ **Thursday** Date _____ All I read today _____

Best thing I marked today: *Reference* _____

Thought: _____

How it impressed me: _____

☐ **Friday** Date _____ All I read today _____

Best thing I marked today: *Reference* _____

Thought: _____

How it impressed me: _____

☐ **Saturday** Date _____ All I read today _____

Best thing I marked today: *Reference* _____

Thought: _____

How it impressed me: _____

MY READING HIGHLIGHTS

"Now, my children, listen to me. Those who follow my ways are happy. Listen to my teaching, and you will be wise. Do not ignore it. Those who listen to me are happy. They stand watching at my door every day. They are at my open door waiting to be with me." —Proverbs 8:32-34 (NCV)

Translation _____ Year _____

☐ **Sunday** Date _____ All I read today _____

Best thing I marked today: *Reference* _____

Thought: _____

_____

How it impressed me: _____

_____

_____

_____

☐ **Monday** Date _____ All I read today _____

Best thing I marked today: *Reference* _____

Thought: _____

_____

How it impressed me: _____

_____

_____

_____

☐ **Tuesday** Date _____ All I read today _____

Best thing I marked today: *Reference* _____

Thought: _____

_____

How it impressed me: _____

_____

_____

_____

☐ **Wednesday** Date _____ All I read today _____

Best thing I marked today: *Reference* _____

Thought: _____

_____

How it impressed me: _____

_____

_____

_____

☐ **Thursday** Date _____ All I read today _____

Best thing I marked today: *Reference* _____

Thought: _____

_____

How it impressed me: _____

_____

_____

_____

☐ **Friday** Date _____ All I read today _____

Best thing I marked today: *Reference* _____

Thought: _____

_____

How it impressed me: _____

_____

_____

_____

☐ **Saturday** Date _____ All I read today _____

Best thing I marked today: *Reference* _____

Thought: _____

_____

How it impressed me: _____

_____

_____

_____

MY READING HIGHLIGHTS

"Now, my children, listen to me. Those who follow my ways are happy. Listen to my teaching, and you will be wise. Do not ignore it. Those who listen to me are happy. They stand watching at my door every day. They are at my open door waiting to be with me." —Proverbs 8:32-34 (NCV)

Translation _____ Year _____

☐ **Sunday** Date _____ All I read today _____

Best thing I marked today: *Reference* _____

Thought: _____

_____

How it impressed me: _____

_____

_____

_____

☐ **Monday** Date _____ All I read today _____

Best thing I marked today: *Reference* _____

Thought: _____

_____

How it impressed me: _____

_____

_____

_____

☐ **Tuesday** Date _____ All I read today _____

Best thing I marked today: *Reference* _____

Thought: _____

_____

How it impressed me: _____

_____

_____

_____

☐ **Wednesday** Date _____ All I read today _____

Best thing I marked today: *Reference* _____

Thought: _____

How it impressed me: _____

☐ **Thursday** Date _____ All I read today _____

Best thing I marked today: *Reference* _____

Thought: _____

How it impressed me: _____

☐ **Friday** Date _____ All I read today _____

Best thing I marked today: *Reference* _____

Thought: _____

How it impressed me: _____

☐ **Saturday** Date _____ All I read today _____

Best thing I marked today: *Reference* _____

Thought: _____

How it impressed me: _____

MY READING HIGHLIGHTS

"Now, my children, listen to me. Those who follow my ways are happy. Listen to my teaching, and you will be wise. Do not ignore it. Those who listen to me are happy. They stand watching at my door every day. They are at my open door waiting to be with me." —Proverbs 8:32-34 (NCV)

Translation _____ Year _____

☐ **Sunday** Date _____ All I read today _____

Best thing I marked today: *Reference* _____

Thought: _____

_____

How it impressed me: _____

_____

_____

☐ **Monday** Date _____ All I read today _____

Best thing I marked today: *Reference* _____

Thought: _____

_____

How it impressed me: _____

_____

_____

_____

☐ **Tuesday** Date _____ All I read today _____

Best thing I marked today: *Reference* _____

Thought: _____

_____

How it impressed me: _____

_____

_____

☐ **Wednesday** Date_____ All I read today _____

Best thing I marked today: *Reference* _____

Thought: _____

_____

How it impressed me: _____

_____

_____

☐ **Thursday** Date _____ All I read today _____

Best thing I marked today: *Reference* _____

Thought: _____

_____

How it impressed me: _____

_____

_____

_____

☐ **Friday** Date _____ All I read today _____

Best thing I marked today: *Reference* _____

Thought: _____

_____

How it impressed me: _____

_____

_____

_____

☐ **Saturday** Date _____ All I read today _____

Best thing I marked today: *Reference* _____

Thought: _____

_____

How it impressed me: _____

_____

_____

MY READING HIGHLIGHTS

"Now, my children, listen to me. Those who follow my ways are happy. Listen to my teaching, and you will be wise. Do not ignore it. Those who listen to me are happy. They stand watching at my door every day. They are at my open door waiting to be with me." —Proverbs 8:32-34 (NCV)

Translation _____ Year _____

☐ **Sunday** Date _____ All I read today _____

Best thing I marked today: *Reference* _____

Thought: _____

_____

How it impressed me: _____

_____

_____

_____

☐ **Monday** Date _____ All I read today _____

Best thing I marked today: *Reference* _____

Thought: _____

_____

How it impressed me: _____

_____

_____

_____

☐ **Tuesday** Date _____ All I read today _____

Best thing I marked today: *Reference* _____

Thought: _____

_____

How it impressed me: _____

_____

_____

_____

☐ **Wednesday** Date_____ All I read today _____

Best thing I marked today: *Reference* _____

Thought: _____

_____

How it impressed me: _____

_____

_____

☐ **Thursday** Date_____ All I read today _____

Best thing I marked today: *Reference* _____

Thought: _____

_____

How it impressed me: _____

_____

_____

_____

☐ **Friday** Date _____ All I read today _____

Best thing I marked today: *Reference* _____

Thought: _____

_____

How it impressed me: _____

_____

_____

_____

☐ **Saturday** Date _____ All I read today _____

Best thing I marked today: *Reference* _____

Thought: _____

_____

How it impressed me: _____

_____

_____

_____

MY READING HIGHLIGHTS

"Now, my children, listen to me. Those who follow my ways are happy. Listen to my teaching, and you will be wise. Do not ignore it. Those who listen to me are happy. They stand watching at my door every day. They are at my open door waiting to be with me." —Proverbs 8:32-34 (NCV)

Translation _____ Year _____

☐ **Sunday** Date _____ All I read today _____

Best thing I marked today: *Reference* _____

Thought: _____

_____

How it impressed me: _____

_____

_____

_____

☐ **Monday** Date _____ All I read today _____

Best thing I marked today: *Reference* _____

Thought: _____

_____

How it impressed me: _____

_____

_____

_____

☐ **Tuesday** Date _____ All I read today _____

Best thing I marked today: *Reference* _____

Thought: _____

_____

How it impressed me: _____

_____

_____

_____

☐ **Wednesday** Date _____ All I read today _____

Best thing I marked today: *Reference* _____

Thought: _____

_____

How it impressed me: _____

_____

_____

_____

☐ **Thursday** Date _____ All I read today _____

Best thing I marked today: *Reference* _____

Thought: _____

_____

How it impressed me: _____

_____

_____

_____

☐ **Friday** Date _____ All I read today _____

Best thing I marked today: *Reference* _____

Thought: _____

_____

How it impressed me: _____

_____

_____

_____

☐ **Saturday** Date _____ All I read today _____

Best thing I marked today: *Reference* _____

Thought: _____

_____

How it impressed me: _____

_____

_____

MY READING HIGHLIGHTS

"Now, my children, listen to me. Those who follow my ways are happy. Listen to my teaching, and you will be wise. Do not ignore it. Those who listen to me are happy. They stand watching at my door every day. They are at my open door waiting to be with me." —Proverbs 8:32-34 (NCV)

Translation _____ Year _____

☐ **Sunday** Date _____ All I read today _____

Best thing I marked today: *Reference* _____

Thought: _____

_____

How it impressed me: _____

_____

_____

☐ **Monday** Date _____ All I read today _____

Best thing I marked today: *Reference* _____

Thought: _____

_____

How it impressed me: _____

_____

_____

_____

☐ **Tuesday** Date _____ All I read today _____

Best thing I marked today: *Reference* _____

Thought: _____

_____

How it impressed me: _____

_____

_____

_____

☐ **Wednesday** Date_____ All I read today _____

Best thing I marked today: *Reference* _____

Thought: _____

_____

How it impressed me: _____

_____

_____

_____

☐ **Thursday** Date_____ All I read today _____

Best thing I marked today: *Reference* _____

Thought: _____

_____

How it impressed me: _____

_____

_____

_____

☐ **Friday** Date_____ All I read today _____

Best thing I marked today: *Reference* _____

Thought: _____

_____

How it impressed me: _____

_____

_____

_____

☐ **Saturday** Date_____ All I read today _____

Best thing I marked today: *Reference* _____

Thought: _____

_____

How it impressed me: _____

_____

_____

_____

MY READING HIGHLIGHTS

"Now, my children, listen to me. Those who follow my ways are happy. Listen to my teaching, and you will be wise. Do not ignore it. Those who listen to me are happy. They stand watching at my door every day. They are at my open door waiting to be with me." —Proverbs 8:32-34 (NCV)

Translation _____ Year _____

☐ **Sunday** Date _____ All I read today _____

Best thing I marked today: *Reference* _____

Thought: _____

_____

How it impressed me: _____

_____

_____

_____

☐ **Monday** Date _____ All I read today _____

Best thing I marked today: *Reference* _____

Thought: _____

_____

How it impressed me: _____

_____

_____

_____

☐ **Tuesday** Date _____ All I read today _____

Best thing I marked today: *Reference* _____

Thought: _____

_____

How it impressed me: _____

_____

_____

_____

☐ **Wednesday** Date_____ All I read today _____

Best thing I marked today: *Reference* _____

Thought: _____

_____

How it impressed me: _____

_____

_____

_____

☐ **Thursday** Date_____ All I read today _____

Best thing I marked today: *Reference* _____

Thought: _____

_____

How it impressed me: _____

_____

_____

_____

_____

☐ **Friday** Date_____ All I read today _____

Best thing I marked today: *Reference* _____

Thought: _____

_____

How it impressed me: _____

_____

_____

_____

☐ **Saturday** Date_____ All I read today _____

Best thing I marked today: *Reference* _____

Thought: _____

_____

How it impressed me: _____

_____

_____

_____

MY READING HIGHLIGHTS

"Now, my children, listen to me. Those who follow my ways are happy. Listen to my teaching, and you will be wise. Do not ignore it. Those who listen to me are happy. They stand watching at my door every day. They are at my open door waiting to be with me." —Proverbs 8:32-34 (NCV)

Translation _____ Year _____

☐ **Sunday** Date _____ All I read today _____

Best thing I marked today: *Reference* _____

Thought: _____

_____

How it impressed me: _____

_____

_____

_____

☐ **Monday** Date _____ All I read today _____

Best thing I marked today: *Reference* _____

Thought: _____

_____

How it impressed me: _____

_____

_____

_____

☐ **Tuesday** Date _____ All I read today _____

Best thing I marked today: *Reference* _____

Thought: _____

_____

How it impressed me: _____

_____

_____

_____

☐ **Wednesday** Date_____ All I read today _____

Best thing I marked today: *Reference* _____

Thought: _____

_____

How it impressed me: _____

_____

_____

_____

☐ **Thursday** Date _____ All I read today _____

Best thing I marked today: *Reference* _____

Thought: _____

_____

How it impressed me: _____

_____

_____

_____

☐ **Friday** Date _____ All I read today _____

Best thing I marked today: *Reference* _____

Thought: _____

_____

How it impressed me: _____

_____

_____

_____

☐ **Saturday** Date _____ All I read today _____

Best thing I marked today: *Reference* _____

Thought: _____

_____

How it impressed me: _____

_____

_____

_____

MY READING HIGHLIGHTS

"Now, my children, listen to me. Those who follow my ways are happy. Listen to my teaching, and you will be wise. Do not ignore it. Those who listen to me are happy. They stand watching at my door every day. They are at my open door waiting to be with me." —Proverbs 8:32-34 (NCV)

Translation _____ Year _____

☐ **Sunday** Date _____ All I read today _____

Best thing I marked today: *Reference* _____

Thought: _____

_____

How it impressed me: _____

_____

_____

_____

☐ **Monday** Date _____ All I read today _____

Best thing I marked today: *Reference* _____

Thought: _____

_____

How it impressed me: _____

_____

_____

_____

☐ **Tuesday** Date _____ All I read today _____

Best thing I marked today: *Reference* _____

Thought: _____

_____

How it impressed me: _____

_____

_____

_____

☐ **Wednesday** Date_____ All I read today _____

Best thing I marked today: *Reference* _____

Thought: _____

_____

How it impressed me: _____

_____

_____

_____

☐ **Thursday** Date _____ All I read today _____

Best thing I marked today: *Reference* _____

Thought: _____

_____

How it impressed me: _____

_____

_____

_____

☐ **Friday** Date _____ All I read today _____

Best thing I marked today: *Reference* _____

Thought: _____

_____

How it impressed me: _____

_____

_____

_____

☐ **Saturday** Date _____ All I read today _____

Best thing I marked today: *Reference* _____

Thought: _____

_____

How it impressed me: _____

_____

_____

_____

MY READING HIGHLIGHTS

"Now, my children, listen to me. Those who follow my ways are happy. Listen to my teaching, and you will be wise. Do not ignore it. Those who listen to me are happy. They stand watching at my door every day. They are at my open door waiting to be with me." —Proverbs 8:32-34 (NCV)

Translation _____ Year _____

☐ **Sunday** Date _____ All I read today _____

Best thing I marked today: *Reference* _____

Thought: _____

_____

How it impressed me: _____

_____

_____

_____

☐ **Monday** Date _____ All I read today _____

Best thing I marked today: *Reference* _____

Thought: _____

_____

How it impressed me: _____

_____

_____

_____

☐ **Tuesday** Date _____ All I read today _____

Best thing I marked today: *Reference* _____

Thought: _____

_____

How it impressed me: _____

_____

_____

_____

☐ **Wednesday** Date_____ All I read today_____

Best thing I marked today: *Reference*_____

*Thought:*_____

_____

How it impressed me:_____

_____

_____

☐ **Thursday** Date_____ All I read today_____

Best thing I marked today: *Reference*_____

*Thought:*_____

_____

How it impressed me:_____

_____

_____

_____

☐ **Friday** Date_____ All I read today_____

Best thing I marked today: *Reference*_____

*Thought:*_____

_____

How it impressed me:_____

_____

_____

_____

☐ **Saturday** Date_____ All I read today_____

Best thing I marked today: *Reference*_____

*Thought:*_____

_____

How it impressed me:_____

_____

_____

_____

PRAYER SHEET

REQUEST	GOD'S ANSWER

PRAYER SHEET

REQUEST	GOD'S ANSWER

PRAYER SHEET

REQUEST	GOD'S ANSWER

PRAYER SHEET

REQUEST	GOD'S ANSWER

PRAYER SHEET

REQUEST	GOD'S ANSWER

PRAYER SHEET

REQUEST	GOD'S ANSWER

NOTES

1. Jim Petersen, *Evangelism as a Lifestyle* (Colorado Springs, CO: NavPress, 1980).

2. At www.2-7series.org, you will find suggestions for locating recent polls and statistics on these issues.

3. Ole Hallesby, *Prayer* (Minneapolis: Augsburg, 1975), 20.

4. Robert Boyd Munger, *My Heart — Christ's Home* (Downers Grove, IL: InterVarsity Christian Fellowship, 1986), reprinted by permission of InterVarsity Press, Downers Grove, IL 60515.

5. Lorne C. Sanny, *How to Spend a Day in Prayer* (Colorado Springs, CO: NavPress, 2008).

CDM ™
CHURCH DISCIPLESHIP MINISTRY

A MINISTRY OF ⬤ THE NAVIGATORS

CDM is a ministry of The Navigators that focuses on helping churches become more intentional in discipleship, outreach, and leadership development. A nationwide network of Navigator staff and ministry partners is available to assist local churches in these areas.

CDM staff often work alongside pastoral staff and church leaders to facilitate the Intentional Disciplemaking Church Process.

It focuses on seven major areas:

- A leadership foundation of prayer, teamwork, and assessment
- Mission, vision, and values clarification
- Spiritual maturity strategy
- Outreach strategy
- Leadership development
- Life-to-life
- Small groups and infrastructure

In partnership with NavPress, CDM continues to develop effective materials for local church ministries.

CDM conducts learning labs where church members are equipped to live and minister in increasing fruitfulness in whatever venue God has placed them.

Ways to contact CDM:

Website: www.navigators.org/cdm
Phone: (719) 594-2446
Address: The Navigators / CDM
PO Box 6000
Colorado Springs, CO 80934